Blue Skies

Military Stories of a Different Kind

**Wing Commander
Sunil Mathews (Retd)
(Mats)**

Cover Designed by – **Arun Joji**

Published and Sold by Notion Press Media Pvt Ltd

I dedicate this work:

To my beloved wife, Gino, who, on the day we tied the knot, vowed to walk hand in hand with me on an unfamiliar and adventurous journey. Your unwavering support and resilience have been my anchor through every twist and turn.

To our treasures, Rohan and Rohit, who filled our home with laughter and energy, braving the unique challenges and sacrifices that come with being military kids—you are our pride and joy.

To my parents, in-laws, and siblings, whose love and encouragement have been my constant source of strength.

And to my countless comrades in uniform, who stood by me like family through every chapter of this extraordinary voyage.

This book is as much yours as it is mine.

PREFACE

A soldier's life is unlike any other—a life of relentless vigilance, unwavering dedication, and unparalleled sacrifice. Soldiers stand as sentinels against threats to our nation, ready to face any hostile situation and, if necessary, lay down their lives for the country they hold dear. Every day for them is a new chapter, brimming with challenges, triumphs, camaraderie, hardships, and even moments of despair.

What sets a soldier's life apart is the very nature of the job— the unpredictability, the diverse and often harsh environments, and the ever-changing faces and tasks that demand quick adaptability. From day to day, they find themselves working in new conditions, interacting with people from different walks of life, and often performing duties that are a stark departure from what they were doing the day before. This constant change shapes them, gifting them a wealth of experiences and stories that are as varied as the landscapes they serve in.

I consider myself incredibly fortunate to have had the privilege of serving my beloved country as a commissioned officer in one of its proud arms—the Indian Air Force. Over two and a half decades, my journey took me across the length and breadth of our vast nation. From the icy cold terrains of the Kashmir Valley to the scorching deserts of Rajasthan, from the dense forests of the North-East to the bustling cities like Delhi and Mumbai, I've witnessed first-hand the extraordinary resilience required to thrive in such diverse and often demanding conditions.

This book is a humble attempt to share a glimpse of that journey. Through these pages, I narrate incidents I have witnessed or been a part of during my service. My focus here is not on the operational aspects of military life—the bread and butter of the armed forces—but rather on the human side of a soldier's existence: the tough living conditions, the camaraderie, and the lighter moments that make the journey worthwhile.

To maintain a light-hearted tone, I have attempted to sprinkle the stories with a touch of humour while intentionally leaving out many of the painful experiences I have encountered.

I hope this book offers readers a fresh perspective on a soldier's life—one that goes beyond the usual imagery of gunfights and bombings often associated with the military. For those who have served in the armed forces and their families, I hope these stories rekindle fond memories of the good old days in uniform. And for others, may it provide a deeper appreciation of the extraordinary life and unwavering spirit of those who serve.

Above all, I hope this book inspires young, passionate men and women to step forward and embrace a career in the defence forces—an unparalleled journey of adventure, purpose, and experiences that no other profession can offer.

DISCLAIMER

This book is solely based on my 25 years of service as a commissioned officer in the Indian Air Force, focusing on aspects beyond our core professional roles. The accounts and perspectives shared here are drawn from my personal experiences and interpretations and may not always align with actual events or widely held views.

The aim of this work is to provide an insight into the tough realities of a soldier's life. It should not, in any way, be taken as an authoritative source or quoted as such. The names used in various chapters are entirely fictitious and bear no connection to real individuals, and any resemblance felt if any are just coincidental.

Some characters depicted in the stories may occasionally display behaviour that does not align with the ideal image of a military officer. This is merely one side of them, as every individual possesses a mix of strengths and weaknesses. It's also important to note that military personnel are a reflection of the broader society, and such rare instances among a small fraction are only human.

Above all, I would like to affirm that I hold the Indian Armed Forces in the highest regard and consider myself truly fortunate to have been a part of the Indian Air Force—the guardians of the skies. Serving that remarkable institution was not just an honour but a defining chapter of my life.

TABLE OF CONTENTS

MILITARY DREAMS

"**B**oom!" The ground quaked as a shell exploded nearby, its deafening roar tearing through the frozen silence of the valley. My heart pounded as shards of ice and dust sprayed into the air. We were lucky—the massive boulder shielding us absorbed the deadly shrapnel. Adrenaline pumped through my veins as we crawled through a jagged crevice, our breaths ragged from the icy climb.

At the ridge, the enemy came into view, mere meters ahead. Their weapons roared, shattering the eerie calm of the night. Instinctively, we dove for cover, our bodies pressed to the frostbitten ground. The sharp retort of AK-47 fire echoed as we retaliated, every shot piercing the dense darkness.

Then came the silence—a moment so sudden and complete it felt very unreal. Only the wind howled, carrying with it the faint whispers of retreat. Peering cautiously over the rock, I caught sight of shadowy figures melting into the night.

Relief washed over me, but just as quickly, pain seared through my leg like a lightning bolt. I fell to one knee, my mind grappling with the sharp, burning sensation.

I opened my eyes to pitch-blackness, disoriented and breathless. My weapon? Gone. My teammates? Vanished. Panic surged. Has the battle ended, or have I slipped into unconsciousness?

I strained to move, and a sudden click jolted me out of my daze. My hand found the cold, familiar object on the floor— the TV remote.

Reality came rushing back. I'd been on the couch, watching a war movie on TV, when the power cut out, and I'd dozed off. My battle? Just a vivid dream. But the sharp pain in my right leg? That was all too real. As I shifted, a jolt shot through me, and I let out a scream. Suddenly, my father appeared in the doorway with a flashlight in hand.

"You've done it again, haven't you?" he grumbled, inspecting my swollen ankle. "Kicked the sofa in your sleep!" His voice was a mix of frustration and concern. I could only let out a scream in response.

That wasn't the first time my imagination had transported me to the frontlines. Dreams of becoming a soldier had haunted and thrilled me since childhood. Like any child growing up, my ambitions changed frequently, shifting as unpredictably as the moods of the sea. Yet, the image of a soldier—standing tall, defending the nation—always lingered, etched deep in my mind.

As I grew older, those dreams gave way to more grounded aspirations. Engineering became my focus, and I found my imagination sparked by circuits and the flow of electric current. Yet, as is often the case, destiny had plans of its own.

During my pre-final year of engineering, a long-forgotten spark reignited. An advertisement caught my eye—an invitation to join the Indian Air Force as an Aeronautical Engineer. It wasn't just a job offer; it was a bridge between my childhood dream and my newfound path.

I sent in my application, unaware that I was about to embark on a journey that would test every ounce of my strength, resilience, and character.

Little did I know, the echoes of my boyhood dreams and the rigors of reality were about to collide, setting the stage for an extraordinary adventure.

A few months later, an envelope adorned with the iconic tricolour roundel of the Indian Air Force arrived by post. Inside was a call letter for the *Service Selection Board* (SSB) interview—the crucial gateway that every aspirant had to pass to earn a coveted Commissioned rank in the forces.

To be honest, I had no clue about that interview process and was eager to learn more about it. Unfortunately, those were the pre-Internet days, when information wasn't available at the click of a mouse button.

While I could have sought guidance from a few of my *'fauji'* relatives serving in various arms of the forces then, I hesitated—I didn't want anyone to know about my attempt, fearing the embarrassment of failure, which I thought was more likely.

My only option was to find a book that would give me a clear understanding of the interview process. After searching through a few bookshops in town, I finally found one that offered a reasonably good overview of the procedures.

In fact, the SSB interview was the second and most gruelling step in the entire selection process. The first step was a written test that assessed proficiency in English, General Knowledge, and the candidate's core area of specialization.

Back in those days, the screening test was conducted before the main interview at the SSB centre itself. Those who failed the screening were immediately sent home, while those who cleared it were allowed to proceed to the one-week long SSB interview.

The process was exhaustive, featuring psychometric evaluations, individual and group obstacle tasks, group discussions, planning exercises, leadership tests, and, finally, the board interview. Even today, it is considered one of the toughest selection processes in the country.

I soon realized that the book could only give a brief insight into the psychological tests, but no amount of training could alter the deeper aspects of human character, which the interview was designed to reveal. Since I was active in sports, I thought the physical and group tasks would be a mere walk in the park.

Two aspects of the process truly terrified me – the group discussion and the board interview. Those days, I was a shy kid —more of an introvert—and even talking to strangers made me anxious. The idea of speaking in front of a group or facing the interview panel filled me with dread. Since I had already decided to proceed with the interview, I knew I had to find a way to muster the confidence I desperately needed to make an impression.

I started making an effort to strike up conversations with everyone I crossed paths with. My colleagues were taken aback by the change they saw in me. I was once the type to avert my gaze, walking past others without acknowledging their presence. On the rare occasions when our gazes met, I would force a smile and quickly retreat like a shadow.

But from that moment on, I made it a point to engage, even finding excuses to talk to my professors—something I had never dared to do before. After a few days of consistent effort, I could feel small but noticeable sparks of confidence starting to rise within me.

My SSB interview was scheduled in Mysore. A day before the interview, I eagerly set off and reached Coimbatore, where I boarded a bus to Mysore.

The bus was packed to the brim, and I clung to the handrails fixed to the roof. The bus crawled along a country road, and after about an hour, I finally managed to find a seat. It was already 7 pm, and I had no idea when the bus would reach Mysore. I wanted to ask my fellow passengers, but none of them understood any of the languages I knew, nor could I make sense of the alien language they spoke —presumably Kannada.

I was scheduled to report at the Mysore railway station at seven the next morning. I could only hope the bus would reach Mysore in time. With my mind wandering over the day's events, I quietly drifted off to a deep sleep.

Much later, I was jolted awake from my slumber by the conductor. He seemed a bit irritated and pointed outside, where I noticed a board that read 'Mysore Depot.' I realized I was the only passenger left on the bus. A quick glance at my watch told me it was 2 o'clock in the morning—far earlier than my scheduled reporting time. I got off the bus, took a rickshaw, and reached the railway station long before dawn.

The small waiting hall at the station was crowded with passengers that night. I noticed many young men around my age and guessed they were all there for the same interview. The next morning, we freshened up and changed into clean clothes, ready well before the designated reporting time.

Exactly at seven, a few military buses in the signature olive green colour arrived in front of the station. After checking our interview call letters, two officers in blue IAF uniforms instructed us to board the buses.

On reaching the SSB centre, we were escorted to barracks and told to be ready for breakfast in an hour. The growling of our stomachs led us to the military dining hall well before the scheduled time. After satisfying our hunger with the first dose of a military breakfast, we were taken to an examination hall for the screening test – the first hurdle we all needed to cross over. An hour later, the results were announced. About forty among us had failed, and a bus promptly took them back to the railway station, right after lunch. The rest of us were relieved to have sailed through the first step unscathed.

For the next few days, we were all busy navigating the interview processes, but we definitely relished the military meals served to us. As I had anticipated, the individual and group tasks, involving physical activity, didn't trouble me at all. I wasn't worried about the psychological tests either, as I knew that even if I tried to fake or be a bit artificial, it wouldn't make any difference. Even the group discussions and the final interview went better than I had anticipated.

On the final day, they announced the much-awaited results. Out of the hundred and twenty candidates who had originally appeared for the interview, only four were selected by the board. To my utter delight, I was one of them.

Having secured a job well ahead of the final year of my engineering course, I was a bit overenthusiastic. In reality, two more obstacles remained before the final selection. The first one was to pass all papers in my engineering course without any backlog. However, I was more worried about the second one – the medical examination.

During my last semester, I was called for the medical examination at the Institute of Aerospace Medicine in Bangalore. I was aware that the military medical examination would be rigorous, and even a minor issue could derail my dreams. I decided not to stress over things that were beyond my control.

However, I was particularly paranoid about one thing – my body weight. I was a skinny, lean figure at the time and worried that I might be rejected for being underweight.

I focused all my energy on gaining a few extra kilos, eating nearly twice my usual amount in hopes of adding some bulk to my slender frame. In the end, it hardly made a difference on the weighing scale.

I knew the medical examination would be exhaustive, involving a comprehensive evaluation of every organ in the body to ensure the candidate was fit as a fiddle before being recommended for final selection.

Usually, those who fell slightly outside the stipulated weight range were required to undergo additional tests and return for evaluation after bringing their weight within the limits. I didn't want to go down that path, as I considered gaining weight an impossible task for me.

On the day of the examination, I arrived at the medical centre with the obvious fear of being underweight. I made sure to have a hearty breakfast beforehand and had packed two large Kerala bananas and a bottle of water, just in case I needed a last-minute swing on the weighing scale.

Just before I was called for the weight check, I hurriedly devoured the bananas and drank half the bottle of water. Perhaps all those supplementary efforts saved me from the embarrassment of being labelled '*underweight*'.

INDOCTRINATION CHRONICLES

While awaiting the final results of my engineering course, another envelope bearing the IAF logo arrived home via speed post. It contained detailed instructions for joining the upcoming batch of the Aeronautical Engineers Course, scheduled to begin training in a month. Following the instructions, I applied for a provisional degree certificate, which the university was required to send directly to Air Headquarters. With that taken care of, I turned my attention to the rest of my preparations.

The list of items I needed to carry to the training centre was quite extensive. It included a medium-sized black steel box—the essential hallmark of a *fauji* on the move—two full-sleeve shirts in Gabardine cloth, a pair of black leather shoes, two pairs of PT kits, bed sheets, handkerchiefs, a necktie, pillow covers, and various other essentials for the training period.

They had emphasized white colour for every item, with the exceptions being the box, shoes and the necktie. I couldn't help but wonder if I was about to join a *'Christian Seminary'* instead of military training centre!

Not many were familiar with Gabardine fabric, and I struggled to find it in Kochi. After much effort, I finally managed to get it from the Raymond shop on MG Road.

Another item on the list had me searching nearly every garment shop in the city—a dressing gown. Such gowns were typically associated with villainous characters in old movies, often portrayed wearing them in dramatic scenes, with a pipe or cigar between their lips. Memories of Malayalam iconic villain actors like *Jose Prakash, Ummar*, and *Balan K Nair* playing such intense roles flashed through my mind. The instructions didn't specify a colour for the dressing gown, but I opted for a white one, fearing that the rest of my white wardrobe might feel overshadowed by a colourful gown!

The days passed quickly, and before I knew it, I was standing at *Aluva* railway station, ready to board the train to Bangalore, where my training would begin the following day.

My parents, siblings, and a few close friends had come to see me off. A wave of sadness washed over me at the thought of leaving my beloved home for the very first time. While bidding goodbye to my father, I noticed tears welling in his eyes. I, too, struggled to hold back my emotions, but I managed to wipe them away with my handkerchief, forcing a cheerful, strong soldier's face for their sake.

As the train crossed the *Marthanda Varma Bridge* over the *Periyar River*, I stood near the door, my gaze fixed on the railway station, now a distant speck. With tears streaming down my face, I stepped back inside and settled into my seat. The compartment was nearly empty, providing me with a quiet refuge to reflect and let the tears flow in peace.

By the time the train pulled into Bangalore in the morning, my homesickness had faded away, and soon replaced by a rising anxiety about the new environment I was about to enter.

In the waiting room, I noticed many young men, scattered around, each having a similar black box that I had. A few were speaking loudly in Hindi. It soon became clear that most of them were from North India – the '*Hindi walas.*' A wave of realization struck me like lightning: 'I would be spending a significant part of my life hereafter, among these Hindi-speaking people.' For a brief moment, the thought of returning home on the next train crossed my mind. But somehow, I gathered my composure and decided to go with the flow. I quietly settled into a corner of the waiting room, distancing myself from those groups.

At sharp seven, a group of IAF officers, in their smart blue uniforms, arrived and instructed us to move out and board the buses. Just outside the station, a fleet of military buses and trucks were waiting for us. We loaded our black boxes and other luggage into the trucks before boarding the buses, ready for what lay ahead.

I had always been fond of the typical Bangalore weather—the crisp morning chill that lingered in the air throughout the day. That morning ride was no exception. After traveling for about thirty minutes, I began to spot buildings painted in a soft ash grey, with the IAF flag flying proudly from flagpoles on the front lawns.

Soon we approached a large iron gate, and above it, in gold-plated letters, the name of the institution was prominently displayed: *'Air Force Technical College'*. It dawned on me that it was to be our home for the next eighteen months. Once we passed through the gate and entered the campus, barracks-like buildings lined both sides of the road.

The bus stopped in front of the first barrack, and an officer began calling out names. A few individuals disembarked there, and the bus continued its journey. Before long, my name was called, and the bus came to a halt in front of another barrack.

As I stepped off, a middle-aged man, who seemed to have been waiting for me, guided me into a room inside the barrack. Although the barracks were old, likely built during the British era, the rooms were kept immaculate, adhering to the military's high standards. Inside, there were two beds, each neatly made with crisp white sheets, and the rest of the furniture was arranged with precision.

Once inside, he took a flask, and poured steaming hot tea into a delicate bone China cup.

While handing over the teacup, he introduced himself. "Sir, I am Chandran. I've been working here as an orderly for the past twenty years."

He spoke in Hindi, assuming I understood it well. Having watched countless Hindi movies, I could follow the language with reasonable ease, though my spoken skills were far from impressive. I was fairly certain he already knew my name, so there seemed no point in introducing myself again.

To break the silence, I gestured towards the second bed and asked, "*Idar kaun?*"

Thankfully, he understood my broken Hindi and explained that the person who was supposed to join with us had opted out at the last moment, so I would be staying alone in the room. That was music to my ears. Otherwise, I would have had to spend the entire training period surrounded by nonstop Hindi conversations, constantly worrying about getting the usage of '*Hei*,' '*Hum*,' and '*Ho*' right in every sentence that I spoke.

Chandran asked the details of my luggage, which I had loaded onto the trailing truck, and went to retrieve it. I had inscribed my name in white paint on the trunk and attached tags to the bags, so it didn't take him long to identify them. By the time I finished my tea, he was back with all my belongings and informed that the new recruits had been asked to report to the auditorium in thirty minutes.

I thought I would go in the casual attire I was already wearing—sandals and all—but Chandran advised otherwise. He suggested I wear a full-sleeve shirt, formal trousers, and black leather shoes. Having observed trainees for over two decades, he clearly understood what was expected of an officer trainee far better than the clueless civilian I had been back then. For the first time in my life, I found myself donning some kind of formal attire, guided by none other than my orderly—my first mentor at the training institute.

By the time I was ready and stepped out of my room, a group of fellow recruits had already gathered outside the barrack. A stern-looking officer in a crisp blue uniform stood a little ahead, shouting instructions for us to follow him. He led us to an auditorium where all the new recruits had gathered.

Scanning the room, I noticed a few Hindi-speaking guys seated in small groups, animatedly chatting. I found myself hoping to spot a few fellow *Mallus* in the crowd. Some of the recruits sported long hair, resembling Bollywood stars, and the way they carried themselves reminded me of a scene straight out of an old Hindi movie set on a college campus.

For the next few hours, we were engrossed in filling out and signing stacks of paperwork. The final set of documents bore a solemn declaration, pledging to serve the nation until our last breath, undaunted by fear or pressure. As we signed, it hit me—we were now officially part of the Indian Defence Forces.

After completing the formalities, we were asked to step outside the auditorium. Gathered under the vibrant shade of a sprawling *Gulmohar* tree, we quickly fell into easy conversations, exchanging stories and forging new friendships.

"Fall in, flights!" barked an officer in uniform, his voice cutting through the chatter. Though most of us had no clue what the command meant, the sudden shift in tone and demeanour of the officers was unmistakable. The friendly guides we had seen moments ago now stood with an air of authority that left no room for questions.

Irritated by our lack of response, another stout officer with a booming voice stepped in, bellowing at the top of his lungs, "Can't you hear, you civilian *kaddoos*! Fall in groups, on the road!" The sheer force of his command jolted us into action, snapping us out of our daze.

It doesn't matter whether you're a fresh recruit or a seasoned soldier—a commanding voice like that is bound to shake you up and dispel any lingering doubts in an instant. We rushed to the road, quickly forming into loose groups.

The officers in blue uniforms stepped in, swiftly organizing us into three neat rows. Those rows were further divided into three smaller groups, each designated as a *'Flight.'* To complete the formation, one member from each group was appointed as the temporary leader, with the title of *'Flight*

Commander'. From that moment on, every movement within the campus was carried out in those '*Flights*,' with the role of Flight Commander rotating among us.

We were ushered straight to the Officers' Mess for lunch, and the sight that greeted us was nothing short of grand. The dining hall was impeccably prepared, exuding an air of elegance as if set for a ceremonial banquet. Tables were adorned with pristine white tablecloths, complemented by sky-blue runners that added a touch of sophistication. The chairs bore white covers, each embroidered with the Air Force insignia, reinforcing the prestigious ambiance.

The table settings were meticulous—plates were placed with precision, flanked by neatly arranged spoons, forks, and knives. Beside each plate, an artistically folded cloth napkin rested, adding a final touch of refinement. Bearers, dressed in full ceremonial attire, stood attentively by each table, ready to serve, embodying the discipline and grandeur of the Air Force.

We were all bursting with excitement, feeling incredibly special as we silently thanked our stars for that great opportunity to join the mighty defence forces. Without wasting any time, we quickly settled into our chairs.

The bearers, standing with precision, motioned for us to take the napkins and place them on our laps. Obliging with enthusiasm, we unfolded the napkins and spread them over our laps—albeit haphazardly, unconcerned if they slid off under the table.

Soon, the main course arrived, and the mouth-watering aroma was enough to make us forget everything else. Without hesitation, the hungry recruits dove into their meals, eager to fill their stomachs.

For the next thirty minutes, we were completely absorbed in eating, paying no attention to anything but the food. Little did we know that this would be our last peaceful meal for a long, long time.

After finishing our first official meal, we exited the dining hall through the rear door, which opened into a charming garden. The garden path led to a large parking lot, at the far corner of which stood a prominent iron gate. Trainees from the senior courses were waiting for us there.

"You *Kaddoos*...", shouted one of them.

Though I didn't understand the meaning of the word '*Kaddoos*' at that time, the tone of his voice and the immediate reaction of my fellow Hindi-speaking recruits made it clear—it was some kind of abuse. The joy and pride we had felt from the lavish lunch evaporated in an instant, leaving us totally deflated.

"What do you think this is? A picnic?" he barked, his voice laced with authority.

"Bloody civilians, get into the flights—now!" he continued, without missing a beat.

The reality hit us like a thunderclap—we quickly realized that life wasn't going to be easy. In an instant, we all scrambled into groups—the so called *flights*. Probably sensing that things were about to get tougher from that point onward, no one volunteered for the role of flight commander.

The same officer who had been yelling at us just moments earlier pointed to a tall guy in the front row and barked, "You, hero! Take charge of the flight!" The rest of us felt a wave of relief, glad it wasn't our turn.

He stepped forward to take charge of the flight. The rest of us stood passively, watching and trying to make sense of everything unfolding before us. He was then instructed to lead us through a few drill exercises.

Promptly, our newly appointed Flight Commander shouted, "Savdhan!"—the very first command heard in every military parade.

Having watched many parades on television by then, we were all familiar with the word and instinctively tried to take up a position we assumed was the 'attention' stance. However, our hands were everywhere, with our legs in a relaxed posture.

"Ba*** C****, what do you think? Are you f****** standing on the MG Road?" shouted another senior.

A few among us, apparently with some prior NCC experience, were performing the drills correctly. The seniors quickly pointed one of them out to demonstrate the correct posture. He executed it flawlessly. However, for those of us who had lived a carefree civilian life until then, it was far from easy. We tried our best, but the seniors weren't shy about shouting at the defaulters and correcting our mistakes. Slowly, there was some improvement, though we were still nowhere near the expectations.

After an hour of drill practice, we marched back to our barracks in our designated flights. Someone from the middle of the formation called out, 'Left – right,' as we struggled to synchronize our steps. It was our first military march, and despite our best efforts, we were far from coordinated.

We reached the barracks and were once again met with a torrent of abuse for the lacklustre march we had just completed.

"Break off now and report back in five minutes, in your PT kits!" echoed another thunderous command.

We hurried back to our respective rooms, each of us consumed by the urgency of the task. I wasn't even sure where I had kept my PT kit and doubted whether I could make it in time. Deep down, I dreaded the possibility of being late—I wasn't ready to be the centre of attention just yet.

However, as soon as I stepped into my room, my anxiety melted away. There, neatly laid out on the sideboard, was my white PT uniform, ready to wear. Next to it on the floor were my PT shoes and socks. Chandran had anticipated the need, expertly unpacked the essentials from my steel trunk, and ensured everything was perfectly set up. His years of experience spoke volumes in that moment.

Grateful for his foresight, I quickly changed into the PT kit and reported back on time.

Once everyone had gathered, the seniors led our flight to the next destination—a place where a pivotal *'fauji makeover'* awaited us!

The destination was a modest shopping complex, designed to cater to the immediate needs of the trainees. At its centre stood the military Canteen Stores Department (CSD) outlet, occupying nearly half the space and serving as the main draw. While the shelves were stocked with a variety of liquor brands, trainees were not yet permitted to purchase any—a privilege that would come later.

Adjacent to the canteen was a thrift shop run by the Air Force Wives Welfare Association (AFWWA). That store stocked an array of essentials, including window curtains, bed sheets, buckets, mosquito nets, PT kits, and even the elusive dressing gown I had struggled to find in Kochi.

At the far corner of the complex stood a humble STD booth, the sole lifeline for communicating with our loved ones back home.

There at the back was a tailor shop, tasked with ensuring our uniforms were tailored to perfection. Beside it stood a cobbler shop, handling all our footwear needs, from repairing soles to replacing hobnails and fixing the heel rims on our drill boots.

Completing the row was a barber shop, where weekly visits were mandatory for all trainees except those of the Sikh faith.

We were given an hour to finish any leftover shopping, provide uniform measurements to the tailor, and complete the obligatory first visit to the barber shop.

The barber shop featured three revolving chairs, each manned by a stern-faced barber clutching a white cloth as if eager to drape it over their next subject. Their expressions were stoic, their movements brisk, and their cheeks bulged with pan, rendering conversation both unnecessary and impractical—any attempt to speak risked an unintentional spray.

Words, however, weren't needed. There was no ambiguity, no discussion, and certainly no room for creativity. The mandate was clear: a single haircut option—the military crew cut. The barbers knew it, and so did we.

One by one, we took our turn in the barber's chair, surrendering to the inevitable. The barbers swiftly draped the white cloth around each neck with practiced ease and got straight to work with their hand-operated trimmers. Thick clumps of hair tumbled to the floor in rapid succession, a silent testament to our transformation.

Within moments, all that remained on our heads was a sparse patch of hair, shaped like an inverted *'Black Katori,'* a stark reminder of the new chapter we were entering.

The barbers meticulously snipped away the stray hairs that remained, using scissors with precision. Next, they applied shaving cream to the back of our necks and around the ear lobes, before using a razor to clear away the tiny stubs. Once the job was done, they quickly wiped our necks and shoulders with a brush, then untied the cloth with a swift gesture, signalling us to vacate the chair. As the cost of that service was deducted from our monthly mess bill, there was no need to waste time on payments.

None of us dared to glance into the mirror, afraid we wouldn't recognize the unfamiliar face now devoid of the thick, dark hair we had grown so attached to.

For those who had once sported stylish Bollywood-inspired hairstyles, the experience was even harder to bear. Many left the barber shop with tears welling in their eyes, grieving the loss of their former selves.

Although the telephone charges soared during that time of day, many of us still used the STD booth to call home, reassuring our families that all was well in our new surroundings.

The hustle and bustle of the shopping complex unfolded at a swift pace, and with everyone moving quickly, we had no trouble completing all our tasks within the allotted hour.

Upon returning, we stood in front of the building, silently scanning each other's faces, trying to recognize those we had become somewhat acquainted with since that morning. It was nearly impossible, as most of us had lost our familiar hair, leaving only faint traces of what had once been there. The seniors taunted us, holding mirrors in front of our faces. Those who had shoulder-length hair before the haircut bore the brunt of the humiliation.

Once the seniors had quenched their thirst for wild satisfaction, they subjected us to a series of physical activities, which they conveniently dubbed the '*military toughening process.*' Often, someone would make a silly mistake, triggering a wave of punishments. Those ranged from simple exercises like '*running on the spot*' to more intense forms, such as '*kneeling*' and '*head rolling*' on the rough, metalled pathways. Bruises appeared all over our bodies, with tiny drops of blood trickling down. Yet, no one paid much attention to the pain. By that point, we had already accepted it as part of the rigorous military training.

That went on for hours, until suddenly, one of the seniors bellowed at the top of his lungs, "Break off! Run to your rooms, take a proper bath, change into your mess dress, and report back in five minutes!"

During the initial briefing, the dress codes had been clearly explained, leaving no room for confusion. If anyone had any lingering doubts, they were too afraid to ask. We all sprinted toward our rooms, some stumbling and falling, but quickly scrambling to their feet, driven by fear, and continuing the race to change.

We had five minutes, and by now, we knew that the run to the room and back to the flight would take about thirty seconds. That left us with exactly four and a half minutes to shower and change into the mess dress—a white, long-sleeved shirt with a necktie, white trousers, and black laced shoes. There wasn't a second to spare.

Anticipating the chaos, Chandran had already laid out the dress. Since I was alone in my room, I managed to get ready in just four minutes.

As I glanced outside, I saw a few seniors waiting impatiently. Eager to show off, I seized the opportunity and rushed back to them well ahead of my colleagues.

Soon, I regretted that impulsive decision. The seniors were waiting for someone to try outsmarting their fellow officers, and I paid the price for doing exactly that.

By the time the seniors were done dealing with me for my overenthusiastic actions, everyone else had gathered. We quickly formed into flights and marched towards the Officers' Mess.

That evening, we were led to the rear gate of the mess, the same place we had assembled after lunch. In the context of any famous battles, there is often mention of the main battleground, and perhaps with that in mind, the seniors had dubbed that spot '*Jhanjatpur*.' Though no war ever took place there, it was our training ground for another battle we fought three times a day—the breakfast, lunch, and dinner.

The seniors would begin by inspecting our turnout: from the precision of our haircuts to the smoothness of our shaven faces, the spotless and wrinkle-free uniforms, and the shoes that gleamed like mirrors. Once the inspection was done, the warm-up exercises for the upcoming battle would commence. Mistakes were inevitable, and when they happened, they were met with both physical and mental corrections. Those who tried to stand out by violating the brotherhood often found themselves singled out for special attention!

Once the preparations for the battle were complete, we would race towards the dining hall, arms raised in a gesture of gratitude to the almighty, shouting a prayer in unison: "*Amma Amma Kana dho... Amma Amma Kana dho...*" (Oh Mother, give us food)

The dining hall retained the same authentic military ambiance we had experienced during lunch, though the waiters were no longer stationed by each table. After hours of intense physical activity, we were starving, each of us eager to dive into the food laid out before us. But we soon realized it wasn't going to be as easy as we had expected.

We wanted to grab the first available chair, but the seniors quickly halted us. They instructed us to stand behind the chairs, and one of them began explaining the various dining etiquettes we were expected to follow. The fifteen-minute lecture covered everything—from how to take a seat like a gentleman to how to open and close the plate, the proper use of cutlery, and even the correct way to leave the table.

Although our growling stomachs screamed for action, fear kept us rooted to the spot. We stood at attention, like true soldiers, and listened intently to the instructions. A demonstration followed, and the session continued for another twenty minutes.

Finally, we were allowed to sit down one by one and open our plates. We tried our best to follow the instructions, but soon realized that executing the actions was far more challenging than listening to them. Mistakes were inevitable, and we had to repeat the steps several times before showing even a hint of improvement.

The waiters began bringing the dishes, and we all instinctively wanted to dive in. But once again, a few more instructions and demonstrations followed. During lunch, the cutlery had been placed beside each plate, but none of us had even spared a glance at it.

"No eating with bare hands. Use the fork, spoon, and knife instead," announced one of the seniors, demonstrating their proper use.

In a way, that was somewhat of a relief, as we hadn't had the chance to wash the dirt off our hands after all the '*war preparations*' at *Jhanjatpur*.

The seniors observed us closely, watching for any slip-ups, and those who made even any were given stern warnings. We could feel their vulture-like eyes on us and knew that we'd pay a heavy price for any missteps outside the dining hall later.

Fear kept us focused, and we tried our best to follow the instructions, though the hunger in our stomachs begged to be satisfied.

Once dinner was over, we were assembled again at Jhanjatpur, where the seniors unleashed their fury, punishing us for all the mockery we did inside. Around ten at night, we were finally marched back to our billets.

We thought the day was finally over and that sleep would soon offer us the relief we desperately needed. But that was not to be. As we returned, a voice bellowed, "Break off! Run to your billets and report back in your PT kits, in *two microseconds*!"

We all dashed toward our rooms. While they used the term '*microseconds*,' we knew it was impossible and assumed it was meant to indicate two minutes, and that's exactly how it turned out. The phrase was just their way of underscoring the urgency of the task. Later, I learned that it was a common practice across the IAF, where commanders would often yell, '*I want this done in two microseconds*'— for tasks that could take hours or even days to complete!

Although it was well into the night, the new recruits had no choice but to change into their PT kits and report back as instructed. A few were unable to meet the two-minute deadline and were made to repeat the process until they could comply with the '*two-microsecond*' requirement.

Then, the real nocturnal activities began—mostly intense physical exercises, with occasional morale lectures and talent shows by volunteers, who soon earned the label of '*jokers*,' providing some kind of entertainment when the seniors grew weary of shouting. The night marches were real fun, often mimicking the famous scene from an old movie, *Full Metal Jacket*, complete with the iconic chant—'This is my rifle, this is my gun...!'

Finally, we were given a break in the early hours of the next morning. Back in the room, fatigue overtook me, and all I wanted was to collapse into bed. We were instructed to report for the health run at five in the morning. I kept the alarm and, without bothering to change out of my PT kit, dropped onto the bed and succumbed to a deep, much-needed sleep.

The morning held even tougher challenges for us, starting with a gruelling ten-kilometre fitness run—a routine that became a mandatory part of every day during our junior term. Good runners from the senior batch led the way, setting a relentless pace. The campus's inner perimeter road formed a circuit just over a kilometre long, and our goal was to complete ten full laps.

Some of the craftier recruits attempted to outwit the system. They would slip behind the sprawling *Gulmohar* trees lining the road during the first lap, only to re-join the group on the final lap, crossing the finish line with the rest. Those clever tricksters knew that their act needed a touch of authenticity and would dramatically feign exhaustion to avoid suspicion.

But the seniors were no fools. Having pulled the same stunts during their own training days, they anticipated such antics and would often conduct surprise roll calls midway through the run. Those caught faced severe consequences, as the seniors showed no mercy in dealing with them. Despite the risks, a few daring individuals repeated the trick, preferring the penalties over enduring the relentless grind of the long-distance run.

In those days, mobile phones weren't existing. To speak with our loved ones back home, we relied on the sole STD booth on campus. The STD rates followed three time-based slabs, with the most affordable rates—just a quarter of the daytime charges—available after eleven at night. Unfortunately, that window was off-limits to us.

Our only option was to make calls during the day when rates were exorbitantly high and a few seconds of conversation could drain our wallets completely!

Hence, we relied on traditional mail—fondly referred to as '*snail mail*' now—to exchange detailed updates with our families.

During our post-lunch assembly at Jhanjatpur, the seniors would appear with all the letters arrived in mail. They would call out names one by one, handing over the much-anticipated mail. However, receiving a letter came with its own quirky tradition.

Those lucky enough to get a letter were required to run around the flights, holding the cherished envelope high above their heads, shouting at the top of their lungs, "*Mera ghar se chitti aaya hai, main khushi se pagal ho gaya!*" (A letter has come from home, and I'm mad with joy!).

Those entangled in love affairs had an even tougher time, as they often received far more letters than the rest! For them, the ritual came with a twist—they had to replace the word '*Ghar*' with '*Mehbooba*'.

While I was eager to hear news from home, the thought of performing such exaggerated theatrics made me uneasy. Every time the letters were handed out, I silently prayed that none would be addressed to me.

Often, the seniors would engage in activities purely for fun. Sundays were designated as relaxation days, with no official training sessions. Trainees were allowed to leave the campus on Sundays but had to adhere to strict regulations regarding dress and timing.

As the newest recruits, we hadn't yet earned such privileges. In the military, they were granted gradually, only after proving ourselves worthy.

On the third Saturday night at the institute, we reported for our usual nocturnal training session after dinner. A senior, clad in combat uniform, came running and passed some urgent information to the others. The panic on their faces was evident, as though something serious was about to unfold.

Moments later, a long siren blared continuously. One of the seniors, still in combat gear, addressed us with a fiery pep talk, concluding with the ominous words, "The time has come to shed blood for the country."

For the next few hours, we crawled, kneeled, and crouch-walked through rough paths, gutters, and corridors in the farthest corner of the campus. It was the moonless phase, and with all the lights switched off, we could see nothing around us. Despite the disorienting darkness, we pressed forward, inch by inch.

After what felt like an eternity, we reached a building we thought we recognized, but the dim lighting made it impossible to be sure.

Then, suddenly, a few lights flickered on, and we realized we were standing in the auditorium — the very same place where we had assembled on our first day. To our surprise, an X-rated movie began playing on the big screen. A wave of relief washed over us. We realized it had all been a prank, a reminder of the lighter side of military life.

All eyes were fixed on the screen, and when the first intimate scene appeared, someone shouted, "You f*****, heads down! You haven't earned the privilege to watch this. It's going to get tough — you need to prove your worth first!"

For the next hour or so, we sat there, occasionally lifting our heads when granted permission to look up. But just as we focused on the screen, a command to lower our heads would come again, before we had a chance to fully take in the scene.

The return journey from the so-called mission was even more gruelling. Many of us sustained injuries to our hands and legs, which the seniors proudly referred to as '*battle scars.*'

Back in front of the billet, the leader of the pack congratulated us all for successfully completing our first *'mission'*.

The leader then announced that he would distribute the wings to acknowledge our success, and we were divided into several groups.

In the IAF, pilots, navigators, and flight engineers wear winged badges on their uniforms—pilots sport full wings, while navigators and engineers have half-wings, with 'N' or 'E' embroidered in the middle.

The badges they assigned to us were to be represented by our moustaches—pilots were to leave a small portion on both edges and shave the middle, navigators were instructed to keep only the left side, while engineers were to maintain the right side of their moustache.

Those of us who didn't fall into either of those categories were instructed to grow a small patch of hair in the middle, resembling the iconic Charlie Chaplin moustache.

After giving us all the necessary instructions, the leader bellowed, "Break off. Report back with your wings in two microseconds!"

Upon reaching our rooms, everyone rushed to shave off the moustaches as instructed, quickly wiped their faces clean, and took a moment to admire their handiwork in the mirror, bursting into hearty laughter before heading back to report to the seniors. A few of us, lacking the requisite manly moustaches, were tasked with inspecting and measuring the wings of others.

We were required to keep our wings until lunchtime the next day, after which we were finally granted permission to shave off the remaining moustaches.

It was the one and only time in my entire life that I ever dared to touch my manly moustache.

SHAPING THE SOLDIER

What I've shared so far pertains to the special training provided by our seniors, which, in fact, was not part of the official curriculum. Yet, they were deemed essential in shaping a soldier's resilience and adaptability and carried on with the tacit approval of the authorities.

While they focussed on inculcating the various cultures and traditions that were the true hallmark of every military personnel, the official training focused on imparting stringent and organized military discipline.

The daily routine consisted of morning PT, parade drill practice, and long, intense theory sessions covering subjects ranging from military strategy to aeronautical engineering. Afterward, we engaged in another round of physical training followed by games in the evening.

Weapon training sessions were frequent, instilling confidence in our ability to handle a wide array of weapons. Additionally, we routinely rehearsed for various ceremonial mess functions, such as *'dining-in'* and *'guest nights,'* which were also integral to the military tradition.

The gruelling physical routines and lack of sleep made it almost impossible to keep our eyes open during theory classes. It felt like we were being trained to stay alert even while half-asleep!

Sometimes, to avoid nodding off, we would engage in whispered, humorous conversations with our closest comrades. I remember one such moment vividly.

During a particularly dull lecture, we decided to play a game where each person had to guess the name of an animal. A friend scribbled *'Frog'* on a piece of paper, which soon sparked a hushed debate whether a frog is considered an animal or not. The ensuing commotion, however, caught the instructor's sharp eye, and we knew we were in trouble.

When questioned, Venky, ever truthful, answered without hesitation, "Sir, we were discussing whether a frog is an animal or an insect."

The instructor, a towering figure both in rank and demeanour, bellowed in a voice that could shake the walls, "Here I am, imparting vital military lessons, and you're debating whether a frog is an animal or an insect?"

The entire class erupted in laughter. The inevitable "Get out!" followed, and we wasted no time in complying, scrambling out of the room with the swiftness of soldiers under fire!

The instructors often conducted impromptu tests to gauge how well we were following the lectures. Unsurprisingly, the results often reflected just how much—or how little—attention we were paying.

One particular test is still clearly etched in my memory. The instructor, without any warning, dictated a few questions and asked us to write our answers on a sheet of paper. Among the questions was one that stumped me completely: Write short notes on '*Empty Section.*'

To be honest, I had no clue what it meant. But rather than leave it blank, I decided to take a creative approach. I filled half a page with a completely made-up explanation, drawing inspiration from the title. I don't remember exactly what I wrote, but it was something along the lines of a section where unnecessary items were emptied!

When the corrected answer sheets were returned, I was in for a shock. It turned out that the question wasn't about 'Empty Section' at all. It was 'MT Section,' where MT stood for Mechanical Transport! The instructor had circled my answer, marked it wrong, and of course, no points were awarded.

Years later, I had the opportunity to work with the same instructor in a unit. One day, I reminded him about my infamous answer from that test. He chuckled but admitted he didn't recall the specific incident. "To be fair," he added, "most of you wrote equally funny answers for the majority of those questions!"

As part of our military training, we were sent on a camp training exercise. We set up tents deep in a remote jungle and spent two weeks learning the essential skills of survival. The purpose was to prepare us for situations that might arise in military life, where such skills could prove invaluable. During those two weeks, we participated in various drills, ate meals prepared in a makeshift kitchen, and slept on carpets, called '*Dharie*,' spread across the floor. The nearby bushes, at a distance from the main campsite, served as our makeshift toilets. For privacy, each of us claimed our own spot, marking it much like wild animals marking their territory, with our 'borders' defined by the natural landscape.

We were divided into two teams – the '*Red*' and the '*Blue*' forces – the so-called attackers and defenders. The objective was to familiarize us with military strategies.

The Red Force would devise plans to infiltrate the Blue Force's territory, doing everything in their power to achieve the mission goals. They would smear their faces with paint, attach small branches to their combat fatigues, and crawl for hundreds of meters to blend into the surroundings.

The Blue Force, on the other hand, would remain vigilant, doing everything possible to prevent the Red team from breaching their defences. It resembled the childhood game of '*Thief and Policeman*,' but with a military twist.

A siren would be sounded to signal the end of the exercise, and everyone would return to camp, where a roll call would be conducted to ensure everyone had safely made it back.

On a fateful day, the drill started in the afternoon and continued well into midnight. Exhausted and eager for rest, we could barely keep our eyes open.

When the roll call was taken that night, one trainee officer from the Red Force was found missing. Instantly, the mood shifted to one of panic. Having spotted a few snakes earlier in the jungle, our fear intensified.

We split into smaller teams and fanned out, combing through the dense jungle. After an hour of relentless searching, one group spotted the missing soldier, comfortably asleep on the branch of a massive tree.

Dressed in full battle gear—his face painted, and branches carefully attached to his jacket and combat helmet—he was nearly invisible. His camouflage had worked so well that spotting him wasn't easy, but our training and instincts kicked in, guiding us to him. It seemed he had been waiting for the perfect moment but had succumbed to the overwhelming fatigue from the day's drills, drifting into a deep slumber. In the end, we were just grateful to find him safe and sound.

A basic survival training was also part of the program. One early morning, we were dropped off in a remote jungle, about fifty kilometres away from the camp.

Dressed in our military combat uniforms and carrying rifles— though devoid of ammunition—it was more of a symbolic gesture. Each of us had a packet of biscuits, a few chocolate bars, and some water in a military-issued water bottle strapped to our belts. We didn't carry any cash.

We were divided into groups of five, and I somehow ended up with four other Malayalee friends. Our task was to navigate the route using the map provided, survive with our minimal provisions, and return to camp. It felt like a competition, with each team eager to be the first to make it back.

We marched for about a kilometre along a jungle trail, eventually spotting some local villagers. Fortunately, one of my friends spoke Kannada and was able to communicate with them. He gathered the directions to a road that led toward our camp. The villagers, showing us great kindness, offered us some '*roti*' and '*sabji*,' which provided much-needed relief to our ever hungry stomachs.

We walked another kilometre and reached the road the villagers had mentioned. Along the way, we spotted a truck carrying freshly harvested millet, and without hesitation, we requested for a lift. The driver couldn't refuse five soldiers in combat gear, with rifles slung over the shoulders.

Whether it was out of respect for the Indian Military, sympathy for our exhausted faces, or perhaps the mere sight of rifles that made him agree, we were not sure. But, in that moment, it didn't matter. All we cared about was reaching our destination quickly and being the first group to finish the task. We had come to realize that healthy competition always added meaning to such activities, making even the toughest challenges feel a little lighter.

We quickly settled atop the hay bundles at the back of the truck. Thankfully, the truck was headed to a location not far from our camp, so we figured the last mile would be the only stretch we'd needed to worry about.

It was fun traveling on top of the truck in our military attire, chatting, singing, and sneaking in some much-needed power naps along the way.

About an hour and a half later, the driver dropped us near the jungle where our camp was located. We realized we had arrived a bit too early—showing up straight away would certainly raise some eyebrows. So, we took shelter under a large banyan tree and dozed off, waiting for a more reasonable time to enter.

Two hours later, we resumed our journey to the camp, confident that no other team would be as clever as us.

However, our hopes were dashed when we arrived at the camp. More than half of the teams were already there. The first group to arrive was made up entirely of North Indian trainees, none of them able to speak even a word in Kannada. Clearly, they had followed the same method we had, but without worrying about the time of their arrival.

That incident made me realize something important: *'language is no barrier when you have the determination to achieve something.'*

Those who fell ill or suffered injuries were excused from all physical training activities, including PT and parade, as long as they could secure approval from the medical officer. However, those who were granted such excuses were required to assemble in a separate group that we titled as the *'Scrounger Flight,'* a name earned because many in that would be feigning injury simply to escape the gruelling physical tasks.

An official punishment known as *'Pack Parade'* was the dreaded consequence for anyone who breached disciplinary norms. The duration of punishment varied based on the severity of the offense—minor infractions like failing to salute a senior could earn two days, while more serious violations, such as sneaking out of campus, could result in as much as two gruelling weeks or more.

Those sentenced to Pack Parade were required to run around the parade ground for an hour each in the morning and evening, fully dressed in their parade uniform, carrying an additional ten-kilogram weight on their backs, and holding a rifle high above their heads with both hands.

The sheer exertion left one completely drained within the first few laps, but the ground training instructors were unyielding, showing no sign of leniency. Enduring the remaining time was a test of sheer willpower—there was simply no way out!

Once, I found myself sentenced to a two-week Pack Parade. It was an experience I'll never forget, though not for the fondest of reasons!

It happened sometime during the second semester at the institute. By then, we were granted permission to leave the campus on weekends, provided we adhered to certain conditions, such as sticking to prescribed timings and wearing the mandatory dress code. The 'book-out' attire consisted of grey trousers, a crisp white full-sleeved shirt, a necktie, a black blazer, and polished formal leather shoes.

While the outfit wasn't particularly bad, it made us stand out unmistakably as trainee soldiers. Walking around the city dressed like that often drew countless stares, especially during the warmer months when wearing a blazer felt far from ideal.

A few among us were regular weekend patrons of the pubs on Brigade Road—an area strictly off-limits according to the book-out regulations. To blend in and avoid undue attention, they would often switch to casual clothing.

Inevitably, some of them would run into instructors during their escapades, leading to swift repercussions. Their actions typically resulted in the cancellation of book-out privileges for a definite period, coupled with the dreaded bonus of at least a week-long Pack Parade.

For those daring enough to break the rules, the risk was ever-present, but so was their penchant for adventure!

During my training period, I rarely ventured out. Instead, I chose to spend my free time indulging in some sports within the campus. The occasional outings I did were typically for specific reasons—either to visit a city restaurant offering Kerala delicacies or to attend services at a local church on Sunday mornings, when I couldn't find partners for my regular sports activities.

One Sunday morning, I decided to attend the service at a nearby church. I didn't want to wear the formal book-out dress; instead, I preferred plain civilian clothes to avoid drawing attention. Many of my colleagues often ventured out in casual attire, and their ease with it gave me the confidence to try it myself.

So there I was, stepping out on my maiden outing in simple civilian clothes—a full-sleeve shirt, trousers, and shoes. It felt refreshingly different.

I stepped out of the campus and began walking toward the bus stop, keeping to the pavement along the roadside. A little farther ahead, in the same direction, was the tennis court.

As I walked, my eyes caught sight of our commandant approaching from the opposite direction on the other side of the road, with a tennis racket dangling from one hand. He was probably heading back to his residence after a game.

The commandant was infamous for being a strict disciplinarian—a figure of dread not just for the trainees but even for the staff. The road we were on was a public street, and given his rank and stature, it was unlikely that he would glance at every passer by. The odds of him noticing me were slim, and even if he did, I could easily pass as an ordinary civilian with no ties to the institute. But my curiosity got the better of me.

The entire time, my eyes were fixed on his face, curious to see if he would glance in my direction. As we got closer, he did look my way for the briefest moment, satisfying my inquisitive mind.

But then, the soldier in me instinctively took over. Despite the road separating us, I snapped into a brace-up salute and called out a loud and clear "Good Morning, Sir," ensuring he could hear me.

He gave a brief nod to acknowledge my greeting and continued walking without sparing me another look. But my curiosity wasn't ready to let go just yet—I couldn't resist stealing another glance at him as he walked away. Perhaps my confidence in saluting had piqued his interest, for he suddenly stopped, turned slightly, and asked, "Which course are you from?"

His question caught me off guard, but it was clear he assumed I was from one of the recent batches that had passed out. I could have easily mentioned a random course number and walked away unscathed. There was no way he could possibly remember every trainee, especially someone as quiet as me.

A small lie would have neatly resolved the situation without any further consequences.

But, my ever-curious nature had other plans. It nudged me to wonder—what might happen if I simply told the truth? Unable to resist, I let honesty take the lead. With a calm voice, I answered him honestly, well aware that I might be inviting trouble.

In an instant, the commander's calm demeanour shifted. He rushed to me, his voice sharp as he asked, "Who gave you permission to go out in this dress?"

I stood there, unable to respond—caught bunking in civilian clothes by none other than the commander himself. He swiftly informed that my book-out permission was revoked and asked me to report to the duty officer straightaway.

As anticipated, I was summoned to his office the following morning and was handed my first official punishment— two weeks of 'Pack *Parade.*'

The routine training and various examinations continued at full throttle, and before we knew it, the first semester was over. After each semester, we were granted a three-week break—the only vacations during those eighteen months when we could truly relax and catch up on sleep.

As we moved into the final semester, we became the senior-most batch, enjoying a few perks and privileges. One of the highlights was the opportunity to train the junior batch, subjecting them to the same rigorous methods we had endured during our first semester.

Once someone joins the forces, they commit to serving until retirement. A very few may not fully grasp the long-term implications when opting for military service at a young age. Later, they may regret their decision and begin doubting their suitability for the tough military life. The rigorous training schedule can amplify these doubts, leading them to consider dropping out of training and leaving the forces.

However, it wasn't that easy. Anyone who deliberately tried to fail the training as an escape faced the risk of having 'Unfit for Professional Employment' stamped on their records. That stigma forced them to seek alternative options.

There were a few in our batch who resorted to unusual behaviour, almost as if they were experiencing psychiatric issues. Over time, that became their ticket out, and they were eventually boarded out, allowing them to withdraw from both the training and the military forces.

Another guy began complaining of severe pain in every joint of his body. Doctors ran numerous scans and tests but found nothing. Despite that, they prescribed him medications, yet he continued to insist on the pain. As a final measure, they encased each limb in plaster, hoping to see the results after a month. Still, he refused to relent, and ultimately, he was medically boarded out.

A week before the passing-out parade, our postings were announced. Those assigned to units in the remote deserts of Rajasthan and the icy regions of Jammu and Kashmir took some time to come to terms with their new reality. Meanwhile, those posted near major cities felt fortunate.

I was assigned to a unit in Gwalior. While I wasn't particularly thrilled about being stationed so far away, I was relieved to know I could easily reach home with a direct train.

The training culminated in a grand Passing-Out Parade. It was time to bid farewell to that remarkable institute, which had transformed a group of civilians into soldiers equipping them with vital military skills and filling their hearts with countless unforgettable memories. We left the institute with pride and an unwavering resolve to fight and sacrifice our lives for the cause of our great nation.

FIRST STATION

We were granted four weeks of leave before reporting to our field units. After relishing the much-anticipated time with family and friends at home, I boarded a train to Gwalior. Though it was my first long train journey alone, I felt at ease, buoyed by the confidence instilled during the training.

A colleague had warned me about Gwalior's brutal summers, where temperatures often soared past fifty degrees Celsius. Thankfully, I arrived during the pleasant interlude between the scorching summer and the biting winter.

The Air Force Officers' Mess, well known as the Residency Mess, was nestled within a grand old palace originally built for the Governor during British rule. Surrounding the majestic building were single-room accommodations for bachelor officers, while a few rooms within the mess building were designated for the visiting officers. I was temporarily assigned one of those rooms inside the mess itself.

The ground floor of the Residency Mess featured a grand dining hall, two charming courtyards, an elegant party hall, a cosy library, and a well-stocked bar. All the guest rooms were located on the first floor. The room assigned to me for the night was distinctly old-fashioned, with a high ceiling, massive doors, and equally large windows, showing evident signs of wear and tear. The light from the high ceiling grew so faint by the time it reached the floor that the room was almost enveloped in darkness.

Though it had been a mini palace decades ago, walking through its dimly lit corridors at night felt a bit scary. Later, during my transfers and temporary assignments to other units, I realized that many officers' messes still operated in such palaces built during the British era.

Having grown accustomed to the moderate climate of Kerala and, for the past eighteen months, the chilly weather of

Bangalore, I found the heat in Gwalior unbearable. Air conditioners were a luxury back then, so the rooms were equipped with desert coolers for some relief. Unfortunately, the high humidity at that time rendered the coolers mostly ineffective. Seeking respite, I spent some time in the bar, enjoying the air-cooled ambiance with a refreshing glass of '*nimbu pani*' before heading for a quick dinner.

Back in my room, I went straight to bed, though I wasn't not sure if it was the heat or the eerie atmosphere of the vintage palace that kept me awake for so long. Lying there, my mind wandering through various thoughts, I eventually drifted off to sleep, much later into the night.

On Sunday morning, I woke up, quickly freshened up, and headed to the dining hall. Over breakfast, I got acquainted with a few fellow officers, one of whom offered me a bike ride into the city. The so-called city was a chaotic jumble, entire construction completely disorganized with no planning or taste. Traffic was a mess, with all sorts of vehicles, carts, pedestrians, and even stray cattle occupying most of the road. The main mode of transport there was the '*Phat Phaties*'—a type of rickshaw, likely named after the distinctive sound of its engine.

We stopped in front of an old building that resembled a faded relic of a bygone era. I realized it was a movie hall only when my friend asked if I was interested in watching the latest Hindi blockbuster starring *Aamir Khan*. With nothing else to do, we decided to go in. Even in the so-called first class, the seats were wooden chairs covered with rexine. The ceiling of the theatre was supported by huge stone pillars placed randomly, obstructing a clear view of the screen from the seats behind them. We often had to adjust our heads left and right to see the full screen.

I began to wonder, 'If this is the state of a so-called city, what might the conditions be like in the more remote areas where most of our Indian Air Force units are stationed?'

MILITARY MESS

The food at the Officers' Mess was unmistakably North Indian, with '*Dal, Roti, and Sabzi*' forming the cornerstone of every meal. Alongside those staples, a non-vegetarian dish, usually a chicken curry or fry, added some variety.

Raw vegetables—cucumbers, onions, and tomatoes—were ever-present on the tables, a nod to the North's love for fresh sides, though to us South Indians, they often felt more like table decorations.

Plain white rice, a comforting staple for rice-eaters like me, made its way onto the menu, likely as a concession to officers from the South. True to Northern traditions, every meal ended on a sweet note. Desserts like '*Gulab Jamun,*' '*Custard,*' or even a simplified version of Kerala's '*Payasam*' (rebranded as '*Kheer*') rounded off the dining experience.

While the menu rarely strayed from that pattern, the taste of each dish often varied depending on the whims and skill of the cook in charge.

Occasionally, the menu featured Chinese or Continental dishes, though they rarely lived up to their lofty names. But no one seemed to mind—a little variety was always a welcome change. A cherished tradition across nearly all Air Force Messes was the Tuesday lunch special: '*Chola, Bhatura, and Ice-cream*'- fondly nicknamed '*CBI.*'

Being a Malayalee, I always savoured delicacies like boiled rice with fish curry, and adjusting to different types of cuisine wouldn't have been easy. However, during the eighteen months of training, I had grown accustomed to a variety of foods and had seamlessly adapted to the fork, spoon, and knife culture.

On weekdays, breakfast was a predictable affair—bread, butter, jam, and a double omelette or a cutlet for vegetarians.

Perhaps that simple yet calorie-rich breakfast was the secret behind a soldier's boundless energy.

Weekends, brought a welcome change, with breakfast featuring North Indian delights like *Aloo Paratha, Channa Kulcha, or Pav Bhaji*. Though they could never rival the flavours of the meals lovingly cooked at home, they had a way of evoking sweet memories and lifting everyone's spirits.

As South Indian cuisine slowly gained popularity in the North, breakfast dishes like *Dosa, Idli, and Uthappam* began to appear on the table. However, we often struggled with the *Idlis*, as the North Indian cooks lacked the skill to make them as they should be.

The sambar, too, was more like a variety of dal with plenty of boiled vegetables thrown in. Since coconut wasn't readily available, the chutney was made by grinding raw chickpeas in a way that mimicked the look, though the taste was far from authentic. Despite those imperfections, the weekend menu was always a welcome break from the usual bread, butter, and jam!

Contrary to popular belief, food in the mess was not free. Every soldier was entitled to a specific ration that covered nearly all essential items for a healthy diet, such as bread, flour, rice, butter, milk, cereals, oil, eggs, meat, vegetables, fruits, and even spices. The mess collected the ration on behalf of all the living-in officers, serving as the primary source of supply.

Additional items were purchased from the local market, with the cost shared among the dining-in members.

Many of the service chefs had undergone training at five-star hotels, with a few even having experience abroad, making them highly skilled. Unfortunately, most of the essential ingredients needed to showcase their expertise were rarely available in the pantry. As a result, they often had to work with basic ingredients like dal, onions, potatoes, plenty of oil, and some ready-made masalas.

However, during parties at the mess, with an abundance of fancy ingredients at their disposal, they had the opportunity to truly demonstrate their calibre.

A catering assistant supervised the kitchen, cooks, and supporting staff, besides managing the rations and other supplies. One of the dining-in members was assigned a role as '*Food Member*', responsible for overseeing all cookhouse functions and deciding the daily menu, with the catering assistant's support. It was an additional duty, carried out alongside their primary responsibilities in the IAF.

At one point, Babu, a colleague from my home state of Kerala, took over as the *Food Member*. A true lover of Kerala cuisine, he had missed it ever since joining the forces. Babu was incredibly innovative, always eager to experiment with new dishes to add to the menu. It was he who introduced *Idli and Dosa* to the mess, much to everyone's delight, quickly earning him many accolades from all corners.

Encouraged by those successes, he pressed on with his culinary experiments, even attempting to introduce 'Puttu'— a steamed rice cake, also a beloved breakfast dish of every Keralite. Unfortunately, he couldn't get the specialized utensils needed to prepare it on such a large scale, and the idea was abandoned.

On Sundays, everyone usually slept in a little longer, often nursing a hangover from the previous night. As a result, most preferred to have breakfast in the comfort of their rooms. Aware of that, the orderlies used to collect the breakfast from the mess and deliver it straight to our rooms.

On a Sunday, during Babu's term as the food member, the orderlies brought breakfast and served it in the rooms, as usual. Everyone was surprised to see four steaming white rice balls on the plate. They resembled *laddus* in shape but were slightly larger and stark white in colour. Noticing the puzzled looks, the orderlies explained that it was a new Kerala breakfast introduced by Babu Sir. Given his past success with

South Indian dishes, everyone was excited and eager to dig in right away.

They took a bite, only to realize it wasn't as soft as they had anticipated. They bit down harder, hoping to break through, but instead, the rice ball clung stubbornly to their teeth, its dense, glue-like texture refusing to yield. After a struggle, they managed to pull it away, eventually tossing it onto the plate in front of them.

The orderly stood by, watching the scene unfold with a bemused expression.

"Take these f****** white cannonballs away! Go feed them all to Babu Sir!" the officers shouted at the poor orderlies in frustration.

Frightened by the officers' furious expressions and harsh words, the orderlies quickly collected the plates and hurried away, eager to escape the scene.

In fact, Babu was attempting to introduce another Kerala delicacy – '*Kozhukatta*', steamed rice balls with a soft, thin outer shell and a juicy coconut and jaggery filling at its core. He tried to explain the recipe to the star chefs using his broken Hindi, but his instructions didn't quite get through. Unfortunately, the chefs made the outer shell too thick. When they steamed it, the exterior turned rock hard while the inside remained uncooked, resulting in a rubbery, unpleasant texture.

Babu's well-intentioned attempt to introduce 'Kozhukatta' ended in failure, and the dish earned the new title of '*White Cannon Balls*.'

Fearing the wrath of his fellow officers, Babu kept a low profile for the next few days, steering clear of them. For a long time after that, he never dared to introduce another South Indian delicacy. In the end, it was their loss—they missed out on the chance to savour a variety of mouth-watering South Indian dishes!

MADHUSHALA

A well-stocked and aesthetically designed bar with comfortable seating was the main attraction of any military mess. The star of the bar was a courteous barman in his pristine white attire, ready to serve any drink you desire—from a simple whisky on the rocks to the complex cocktail '*Ramos Gin Fizz.*'

Having a bar in the mess does not mean that every *fauji* was a binge drinker. The majority were non-drinkers or occasional drinkers at most. Yet, they always enjoyed the lively and relaxing ambiance of the bar in the evening, sipping on juice or soft drinks, while listening to nostalgic songs or engaging in lively discussions with their colleagues.

In those days, only the bar and party halls had air conditioners. During summer evenings, the bar was invariably crowded as everyone flocked there to enjoy the cool air. Actually, it was the place where everyone found solace to chill and relax after a stressful day at the office.

In the forces, rank and seniority counted a lot. In the high-stress military work environment, it was common for seniors to lose their temper and burst out at their subordinates. Juniors had to swallow their pride and listen to their seniors, rarely getting a chance to voice their side in the volatile and tense environment. Although most issues were typically resolved later in the office itself, the relationship often remained somewhat strained.

It was customary for the senior to invite the dejected junior to the bar in the evening to ease the tension over a drink. That often led to a healthy discussion, and by the end of it, the tension would have melted away, restoring the cordial relationship.

On my second evening in Gwalior, I went to the bar primarily to escape the hot and humid weather. An elderly group was gathered in one corner, watching TV and occasionally sipping from their glasses. Another young group was on the sofa discussing the latest Bollywood movie, which I had watched a few hours earlier. Most of their conversation revolved around the heartthrobs of that era: *Karishma, Juhi, and Raveena*. Though I wanted to join in, I wasn't familiar with anyone in that group. So I decided to take a bar stool right in front of the counter and ordered a fresh lime juice.

A little while later, an old man, apparently in his seventies, walked into the bar. From his age and appearance, I presumed him to be a retired officer. Everyone in the bar greeted him with a customary 'good evening,' and I followed suit.

"*Pandeyji, kya haal hai?*" he inquired the barman, who acknowledged the new guest with a traditional '*Namaste*' and immediately began preparing a drink for him without needing to be told.

Later, I realized that most barmen possessed a unique quality: once they prepared a drink for an officer, they remembered it forever. They knew precisely when to serve the next drink and the officer's usual capacity too. I experienced it myself in a bar years later and always marvelled at how they could remember all those details so accurately, even after a gap of so many years!

I noticed the young group, previously engaged in an animated discussion, suddenly go quiet. A few even hurriedly left the bar. After picking up his drink, the old man seated himself on the bar stool next to me. Hesitant to start a conversation, I simply looked at him and smiled.

"Hello, young man. Are you newly posted here?" he asked, adding an extra emphasis to each word, perhaps to underscore his veteran status.

I introduced myself, and he responded by recounting his entire service life in a not-so-brief introduction. As I had guessed, he was a distinguished veteran who had served during both the Indo-Pak wars. Meanwhile, the entire crowd in the bar had vanished, except for one person at the far end who was glued to the news on CNN channel. A few officers gave me sympathetic smiles as they left, which I didn't understand.

He then pointed to the now vacant sofa and suggested, "Come, let's sit comfortably on the sofa."

We moved to the sofa, and he began recounting his endless adventures in uniform. Initially, I found it all interesting, but as the monologue continued endlessly, I started to grow bored. He seemed unconcerned whether I was listening or not, but out of courtesy, I interjected with occasional *'wow'* or *'that's great, sir'*. Perhaps encouraged by my responses, he delved into describing his heroism during both the wars.

Pandeyji dutifully served him drinks at regular intervals. Nearly two hours passed like that, during which he had consumed four or five drinks. Throughout, I silently hoped someone would enter and provide me with an opportunity to escape the ordeal, but no such luck befell on me.

Finally, as closing time approached, he departed on unsteady legs, mumbling a 'Good Night' to me.

Since that incident, I became cautious when visiting the bar, always ready to make a swift exit at the first sign of any such old gentleman on the horizon.

The bar sometimes witnessed amusing situations as well. On one occasion, a team of officers from another unit arrived on a temporary duty at our station. Among them was a Malayali officer whose uncle happened to be a famous South Indian movie actor. He was so proud of this connection that he made it a point to announce it to everyone he met in the mess.

One weekend, a movie starring that very actor was being aired on Doordarshan. The officer, along with his friends, made such a racket that it caught everyone's attention. Before the movie even began, the entire crowd had gathered at the bar. *Pandeyji*, delighted to see the bar full, eagerly served drinks to everyone. Meanwhile, all eyes were glued to the officer sitting on the sofa, his status as the star of the evening clear for all to see.

The movie began, and soon enough, the star appeared on the screen dressed in a safari suit. The officer's allies cheered loudly. A Malayali colleague of the officer provided live translations of the dialogues into Hindi for everyone's benefit.

However, after a few minutes, the hero character turned into a villain, and the scenes that followed included several lengthy rape scenes.

Perhaps due to the unfamiliarity with classical Malayalam movies existed at the time, Malayalam cinema generally wasn't highly regarded among the North Indian audiences and was often dismissed as mere masala fare filled with naughty scenes.

Probably, that notion led the audience to assume that the movie was another masala film and to view the actor from that perspective. All eyes quickly turned back to the officer, that time with obvious sarcasm. Clearly uncomfortable, the officer quickly disappeared long before the movie ended!

At times, the bar has even played a role in saving lives.

Winter months in the North can be extremely harsh, with night temperatures often dropping below zero degrees. One such winter evening, we all gathered at the bar to warm ourselves with something hot.

After an hour or so, we decided to call it a night before the cold worsened. For some strange reason, my friend Santy wanted to have a few more drinks and stayed behind at the bar while the rest of us moved to the dining hall.

By the time Santy finished his drinks and came to the dining hall, we were already back in our rooms, preparing to get under the quilt.

A few minutes later, we heard a deafening explosion and rushed outside to see what had happened. It didn't take long to realize the sound had come from Santy's room, so we rushed there to check.

The front door was almost unrecognizable, severely damaged and barely hanging on its hinges, as if it could collapse at any moment. Inside the room, the scene was pure chaos—puddles of hot water scattered everywhere, the bathroom door shattered into pieces and piled up in a far corner, and the bed soaked in boiling water, steam rising from it.

We frantically searched for Santy everywhere inside the room and around, but he was nowhere to be found.

Just when we were starting to panic, Santy strolled in, blissfully unaware of the chaos around him. A wave of relief washed over us—thankfully, he was unharmed.

He casually mentioned hearing an explosion while in the dining hall but had no idea it had come from his own room!

We quickly turned our attention to the room and soon discovered the culprit: the geyser. To ensure hot water was always available, he had a habit of leaving the geyser on throughout the winter.

With all the safety mechanisms failing, pressure quietly built up inside the geyser. Eventually, it reached its limit and exploded with a violent bang!

The explosion was so powerful that it sent debris flying all over, shattering the door into pieces, creating a scene straight out of an action movie.

Had Santy not decided to stay back at the bar a little longer that evening, he would have been in bed when the incident happened. He could have probably suffered serious burns or, worse, been struck by the flying debris.

Fortunately, nothing happened to him—all because he chose to linger in the bar and have a few extra drinks that evening!

BACHELOR LIFE

In the forces, the marriageable age was twenty-five, so those who joined earlier inevitably began their journey as bachelors. Those were the golden years—young officers, full of energy, embracing independence, and indulging in all sorts of mischief. With the right friends around, it was pure, unfiltered fun.

There were hardly any avenues for entertainment back then— no internet, no mobile phones. The only solace was a television in the mess, offering a handful of Hindi channels and news broadcasts.

Weekends for bachelors were mostly nocturnal, much like an owl's. Sometimes, it could be a night ride around the city, a barbeque party in the mess, or a spirited cricket match on a Saturday morning.

Bachelors had the freedom to bounce on married officers, even late at night. They were considerate enough to avoid officers with small children or those living with elderly parents. Usually, the primary targets were newlywed couples who had just moved into a quarter.

The purpose was simple: to enjoy some drinks, food, conversation, and have fun. They would help the lady prepare something with whatever ingredients were readily available, then enjoy it together with nonstop chatter and jokes. Many of the ladies, who perhaps had never cooked before marriage, saw those spontaneous gatherings as an opportunity to experiment and improve their cooking skills.

During such escapades, they were wise enough to steer clear of the senior lot—not out of deference to their rank, but to dodge the inevitable monologue filled with endless tales of past glory, often revolving around their youthful heroics.

Another troublesome bunch were the binge drinkers—those who simply wouldn't let you leave after just one drink. To them, stopping at one was a bad omen, and they'd often insist, "If I offer you just one drink, it's as good as poisoning you. You have no choice but to have at least one more!"

Once, during a *'bouncing'* adventure, we found ourselves in an awkward situation. After watching a late-night movie at the mess, no one was eager to hit the bed early. Someone suggested going for a stroll, and everyone agreed. After a few minutes, we arrived at the area where the married quarters were located.

A senior officer from another unit had recently moved in, and none of us knew him well except for the leader of our pack. He suggested we bounce on him and have some fun. Though reluctant, the rest of us eventually agreed.

The officer was obviously asleep and likely not so thrilled to see a few strangers at that hour. However, our leader boldly announced that we were there for a drink. For tradition's sake, our presumed host did not object and promptly welcomed us. The two of them engaged in some conversation that the rest of us weren't interested in. We quickly grabbed a drink and prepared to leave.

But our host made it clear we couldn't leave just yet, saying, "Coming over was your choice, and leaving will be mine."

He then poured drinks for everyone. With no way to escape, we stayed, listening to his monologue and occasionally sipping from our glasses. That went on until four in the morning, when he finally did let us go. It was a lesson we wouldn't forget, and from then on, we never dared to venture into unfamiliar territories again!

One by one, the bachelors would get married and move out of the group. There was a tradition of welcoming the newlywed couple upon their arrival, led by the bachelor group. Though the officers knew that their colleagues would hatch some plan, they were prohibited from forewarning their spouses. Even if they did, the resourceful bachelors always came up with something innovative.

On the day the newlywed couple arrived, nearly all of the officers' colleagues, including a few married officers with their spouses, would show up at the railway station. While the welcome introductions were going on, someone in uniform would approach and hand a copy of a '*signal*' to the newlywed officer.

The '*signal,*' similar to an old telegram, was used by the military for communication between various formations. The one just handed over, of course concocted by his colleagues, and would typically contain an immediate posting order to some remote location or a temporary attachment to a distant unit for an official commitment.

The officer would quickly brief his wife about the urgency of the situation, promising to return as soon as possible, and then leave immediately. Before the lady could fully grasp what was happening, he would have already vanished. The other ladies would then take over, beginning the act of consoling her. They would move to the Officers' Mess, where she would be accommodated in the guest room.

The welcome group would spend time with her, supposedly to cheer her up. They would engage in various conversations, some about an officer who went on a similar duty and hadn't returned even after three months, or about someone who went to a similar place and sustained battle injuries. Those frightening stories were intended to unsettle the young bride. No matter how strong she was, the setup was usually enough to bring her to tears.

If the initial stories didn't work, the intensity of the acting and storytelling would increase, becoming more animated and creative until the breaking point.

After hours of apparent tension and suffering, the Commanding Officer (CO) and his wife would finally arrive. At the sympathetic request of the ladies, the CO would intervene and issue orders to bring the officer back immediately by any means necessary. Soon, the officer would return, embrace his wife with a bit of drama, and they would happily commence their military journey together.

Sometimes, the prank would involve accusing the officer of cheating. One of the ladies in the group would make an appearance, pretending to be his first wife, even showing edited photos as proof. The group would split into two, feigning support for both the newlywed wife and the woman claiming to be married to him. Some would add fuel to the fire by sharing embellished stories of his past romantic affairs. After creating enough commotion, the woman who claimed to be married to him would finally appear with her actual husband and child, clearing up all doubts.

Often, a few members of the gang would dress as dacoits, ambushing the couple midway, and take them somewhere a bit far away, staging an elaborate drama. Whatever the prank, everyone would cooperate, dress appropriately for the occasion, and act convincingly, ensuring the young bride's introduction to the military community was memorable.

At times, their acting would land the gang in trouble, especially when they staged their performances in public places on the outskirts. Unsuspecting villagers, witnessing the commotion, would often mistake it for a real incident— believing the lady was genuinely in distress. Some would step in to intervene, while others would call the civil police. That was the team's signal to drop their disguises and make a quick escape before things spiralled out of control!

It wasn't just about fun! By the time all the theatrics were over, the young bride would have met everyone in the unit, settling in as if she had found a second family. That deep sense of camaraderie was the heart of military life—where strong bonds between families weren't just cherished but essential for navigating the challenges of remote postings and harsh living conditions.

HOPE

In the early nineties, women began joining the defence forces in the administrative and engineering streams, marking a significant shift in what had long been a male-dominated realm. There was some uncertainty about how they would adapt to the tough military environment.

Commanders of the units selected for their initial induction faced considerable challenges and had to quickly implement the necessary infrastructural changes for a smooth and successful integration.

It was a challenging time for the male folks too, as close scrutiny often curtailed their absolute freedom in many ways. However, the bachelor officers were excited about the prospect of having a few female colleagues joining them. Unfortunately, only a few units were chosen for the induction of them from the initial batches.

The bachelors in the unlucky units remained hopeful, praying for the next batch to bring some women officers to their units as well.

On a Friday evening, most of the bachelors were at the bar when another one walked in, his face beaming with joy. Everyone recognized the paper he held prominently in his hand: '*a signal copy*'.

Posting signals usually arrived on Friday evenings, and they all guessed it might contain one of their posting orders. A few, who were due for transfer, felt a shade of anxiety.

The one holding the signal wasn't in a hurry to disclose its contents. Some tried to snatch it from him, while others begged him to read it out.

After enjoying the commotion for a while, he finally began to read it aloud. *"Pilot Officer (Ms) Renu posted to Air Force Station .... with effect from ....."*

It took a moment for the news to truly sink in. Those who couldn't quite believe it grabbed the *signal* from their colleague and read it for themselves. In an instant, the bar was filled with a celebratory mood, the air buzzing with jubilant energy that seemed to sweep everyone up. Pandeji found himself in the thick of it, working tirelessly to keep up with the soaring demand for drinks that evening.

They had been eagerly awaiting that moment for a long time and thanked the higher authorities for answering their prayers. Almost all of them memorised the joining date mentioned in the posting signal.

The entire conversation in the bar that day revolved around the posting signal. A few speculated about what their soon-to-be colleague might look like.

"She's slim and beautiful," claimed one confidently, quickly adding "I guess" when he noticed others staring at him.

Few others started wondering which state she might be from. A Malayali friend suggested she might be from Kerala, noting the commonality of that name there. A Punjabi disagreed, mentioning its prevalence in many parts of the North. Another person pointed out that '*Renu*' was common in Maharashtra, citing the example of the popular TV star *Renuka Shahane*, who gained fame with the show '*Surabhi*' during those days.

Unfortunately, the surname was not mentioned in the signal with her name, so no definitive conclusion could be drawn.

The day before her expected arrival, the bachelors were anxious. They had anticipated her to arrive at the mess, as was customary for timely reporting the following day. However, their wait proved futile.

"Has the posting been cancelled?" wondered one guy.

"Hey guys, let's not be pessimistic. Can't we show patience for one more day?" a wise man questioned their impatience. Everyone fell silent.

"If she doesn't report tomorrow, we'll ask the Adjutant," he added. Though they wondered who would dare to do so, they kept their hopes alive.

The next morning, a few of them donned their best uniforms, perfectly starched and ironed, with shoes polished to a mirror-like shine. Ready for action, they set off on their mission. They arrived at the Adjutant's office, pretending to check documents and fill out forms. Since anyone arriving on postings had to report to the Adjutant first, they hoped to catch sight of *Renu* there.

They spent nearly an hour pretending to attend to their tasks, but *Renu* was nowhere to be found. Too embarrassed to ask the staff directly, they lingered around, exchanging quiet glances and hoping for any update that might shed light on her whereabouts.

The Adjutant noticed the unusual rush in his office and called one of them over to inquire. The young officer claimed he was there for checking something in his personnel documents. However, during the conversation, he inadvertently spilled the beans by mentioning the posting signal.

The Adjutant understood the reason behind the commotion, smiled at the young officer, and decided to stir up his anxiety a bit. "She reported here yesterday," he said.

The officer couldn't believe it. How could she have reported without anyone noticing? It didn't seem possible. He looked at the Adjutant, confusion plainly evident on his face.

The Adjutant suppressed a laugh and quietly added, "In the Dog Squad. Pilot Officer (Ms.) Renu is a trained sniffer dog, a German Shepherd."

He quietly left the Adjutant's office and spread the word to all his partners in crime. That was when the group realized that sniffer dogs in the military dog squad were also given officer ranks, just like their human counterparts!

A SALUTE GONE AWRY

In the defence forces, saluting is the formal method of greeting. It is mandatory for juniors to salute their seniors, and equally important for seniors to acknowledge and return the salute.

A standard salute is performed while in uniform and wearing headgear. If headgear is not worn, a different form known as the *'Brace Up Salute'* is used. Although the saluting rules were similar, the methods vary slightly between the three branches of the forces: the Army, Navy, and Air Force.

In offices, it was sufficient to salute a senior once when you first see them in the morning. However, some individuals choose to salute every time they pass a senior in the corridor. Conversely, a few may try to avoid saluting by pretending to be on the phone or engrossed in reading a file. If such behaviour occurs frequently, the senior may initiate disciplinary action, leading to an inquiry and subsequent remedial measures.

There is a famous story related to it. It is said to have happened some time ago in an Army unit. Once a junior officer approached the commander with a complaint that a havildar always avoided saluting him. Upon investigation, the commander discovered that the officer never really bothered to return the salutes.

The commander swiftly decided on a punishment. He ordered the defaulter to give the officer five hundred salutes. The officer was pleased and stood by, counting the salutes as the havildar began. Then the commander intervened. He issued a stern warning to the officer and instructed him to return each salute he received.

For the next half an hour or so, both stood at attention, busy saluting and returning salutes. That might be just a story, but it highlights the importance of returning a salute.

Saluting sometimes led to hazardous situations as well. A senior officer learned this the hard way.

He was the administrative head of a forward unit, overseeing matters such as messes, accommodation, camp hygiene, security, discipline etc. Every evening, he took long walks within the expansive campus, primarily to inspect the remote facilities.

There was a unit of Dog squad, located a bit far from the main office building, towards the far end of the campus. One day, the administrative head chose the stretch in front of the Dog Squad for his evening walk.

From a distance, he saw the dog handler training a German shepherd. The handler was so engrossed in his work that he didn't notice the senior officer approaching.

The admin head realized that and, when right in front of the gate, made a customary query to the handler while still walking, "Sab thik hai na?"

That's when the handler actually noticed the senior officer. He quickly came to attention, saluted, and loudly uttered, "*Jai Hind, Sir.*"

The dog saw the handler lift his hand sharply and thought it was an instruction for him. It quickly ran after the administrative head, who had walked a few steps ahead by then, and pounced on him from behind.

Luckily, the vigilant handler recovered from his initial shock and responded quickly. He ran after it, grabbed the dog's collar, pulled him away, and instructed him to stay still. The dog promptly obeyed and sat down as if it were just another training session. Thanks to the handler's quick intervention, nothing much happened except for a reasonably good bite on the right bum of the administrative head.

A simple salute was probably the trigger for all that drama. Whatever it was, the administrative head had a difficult time for the next few days, unable to sit properly and having to take the stipulated dose of rabies vaccine!

RAJEEVAN SINGH

Discipline is of utmost importance in the defence forces, distinguishing the soldiers from others. Everything from their dressing, behaviour, and walk to performing tasks with full enthusiasm represents different facets of discipline. Those habits, instilled in every soldier, last a lifetime. The saying '*Once a soldier, always a soldier*' perfectly captures it.

However, since soldiers come from the broader population, where all kinds of personalities exist, there are bound to be a few troublemakers. In the defence forces, where everyone is under constant scrutiny, such indiscipline rarely goes unnoticed and is eventually dealt with. Yet, there are always a few who know how to bend the rules to get what they want, even when they aren't entitled to it.

While posted at a field unit, I was busy with some files one morning when a Corporal walked in. He saluted and introduced himself, "Sir, I am Corporal R Singh. I have been told to report to you."

I remembered the adjutant informing me that he would be sending someone to my section. I acknowledged his salute with a 'Jai Hind' and told him to sit down.

From his turban, I immediately recognized that he was a Sardar. Having worked with many Sikh colleagues over the years, I noticed something unusual right away. His turban looked different – more of a ready-to-wear type. Sikhs generally sport long beards, but this guy had a thick, neatly trimmed beard and a striking handlebar moustache.

As I was busy with some important work, I quickly inquired about a few service-related matters, then asked him to report to my deputy for the rest of the formalities.

My initial doubts were further strengthened during that conversation. Every Sardar I had met loved to speak in Hindi, so I asked all my queries too in Hindi. Surprisingly, he replied in English with an unusual accent. However, being busy, I decided not to ponder it any further.

That evening, while walking back from the football ground, a young man with neatly trimmed hair and a finely groomed beard came running toward me.

"Good evening, Sir. Do you recognize me?" he started the conversation in fluent Malayalam.

I knew I had seen him somewhere but couldn't recall where. Since beards were not permitted in the forces, I guessed he wasn't from the military. Yet, sensing a hint of familiarity, I hesitated to admit that I couldn't quite place him.

"I am Corporal R Singh," he added, sensing my dilemma. I was certain I had never met a Malayalam-speaking Sardar. Enjoying my confusion, he continued, "Rajeevan Singh, Sir. I reported to you this morning."

I remembered meeting him in the office. Yet, I was surprised by his fluency in Malayalam. I had a colleague, Abdesh Jha, originally from Bihar but born and raised in Trichur, who spoke Malayalam fluently.

Anticipating a similar backstory, I asked "Rajeevan, you speak Malayalam so fluently. How did you learn it?"

"Sir, I'm originally a Malayalee. My given name was Rajeevan, but I converted to Sikhism and adopted the name Rajeevan Singh," he explained.

That cleared up many of my doubts from that morning but only heightened my curiosity about what had led him to do that. Thankfully, he soon began to tell his story.

He had been a football player since his younger days and played at the district level. He continued playing for the university during his degree course and was doing really well.

In the meantime, he was selected for the Indian Air Force. Had he waited a little longer, his sports achievements could have easily secured him an impressive position in the state police department.

However, his well-wishers urged him to join the forces, believing it would provide him with an opportunity to play at a higher level and potentially make inroads into the national football team.

Soon after joining the forces, he did find a place in the IAF team. However, life wasn't easy, as many talented footballers from football-crazy states like West Bengal, Punjab, Goa, and his own state, Kerala, were eagerly waiting for their chances. Despite his best efforts, he couldn't progress beyond being a reserve player in the IAF team.

I listened quietly, piecing everything together and still wondering what had led him to embrace Sikhism. Truthfully, I have always admired the Sikh faith and often told my friends that if I were ever to change my religion, it would be to Sikhism. I thought perhaps he had felt the same pull as well.

He looked at my face, likely reading my thoughts, and continued his story.

Since his football aspirations were not going as planned, he became frustrated. That's when he decided to grow a beard. Back in those days, long beard was a trend among all the heartbroken guys in Kerala.

In the service, growing a beard was considered a sign of indiscipline. Permission to keep a beard for short periods were granted only in very exceptional circumstances, typically on medical or religious grounds. Yet, he requested permission, only to have it promptly denied.

That's when someone joked that he could convert to Sikhism and grow a beard without needing any approval. He took it seriously, followed all the procedures, converted to Sikhism, and adopted the new name 'Rajeevan Singh'!

At the office, he wore his turban with the dignity befitting his faith, but outside, it was a different story. He would stroll around without a turban, sporting neatly cropped hair and confidently flaunting his impeccably groomed beard!

PRESCRIPTION PUNCH

Every military unit has small dispensaries to address urgent medical needs. A doctor assigned to the unit is the first person every sick individual meets. Most cases are treated on-site. In addition to attending to the sick personnel including families, they are also responsible for conducting routine medical check-ups besides promoting medical awareness and camp hygiene. If further examination or care is necessary, the unit doctor refers such cases to the nearest Military Hospital.

Super specialty hospitals located in major cities have comprehensive facilities and handle medical needs beyond the capabilities of the military hospitals. Those hospitals employ doctors with super-specializations and many years of experience in respective domain.

All of them are military doctors holding commissioned ranks, just like any other officer in the forces. The only difference is that they adopt the equivalent rank and uniform of the new service arm when they get transferred between the Army, Navy, and Air Force units.

Generally, most military doctors tend to maintain a serious demeanour, especially while on duty, perhaps to prevent patients from getting too friendly and feigning illness to avoid the tough military routine.

However, there are always a few who exhibit wit or adopt extra ordinary and at times slightly funny treatment methods.

While posted at Gwalior, I had a colleague named Venu, who was newly married at the time. His wife, being a typical Keralite, found it challenging to adapt to the military lifestyle. Even the few hours he spent away at the office were a struggle for her, as she wasn't yet accustomed to being apart.

One day on his way to the office, Venu's scooter had a minor collision with a bike coming from the opposite direction. He felt an unusual pain in his right palm and decided to go straight to the station clinic. Whether the pain was genuinely severe or exaggerated through his fine acting skills, the doctor was unsure. Not wanting to take any chances, the doctor decided to determine if there was a fracture. Unfortunately, the clinic did not have an X-ray facility, so he was referred to the nearby Military Hospital (MH).

Thinking his wife would worry, Venu decided not to inform her at that moment. The MH, Gwalior was just a few kilometres away, and he thought he could explain everything in person when he returned. To his bad luck, the X-ray at the MH revealed a fracture in his right middle finger.

Another issue then arose: the orthopaedic surgeon was unavailable, and Venu was referred to MH Agra, about 120 kilometres away, for the surgery. That's when Venu became concerned and wanted to inform his wife but was unsure how she would react. Still hoping to return by evening and explain everything in person, he called me and asked if I could inform his wife that he wouldn't be coming home for lunch and might be a little late due to some urgent work in the office. I promptly relayed his message.

There were more trouble for Venu in the store. He could reach the MH only after the normal working hours, and his case being not an emergency, they admitted him there and posted the case for the next day. Having no other way, he called up his wife and informed her everything adding that it was just a small fracture and he would be back the next day.

Orthopaedic surgeon examined him the following day, but due to the swelling, they decided to wait until it subsided, prolonging his stay in the hospital. When Venu explained the situation to his wife, she feared there was something more serious that everyone was hiding from her. She demanded his immediate return, causing considerable panic and concern among us all. We approached the medical officer with a request to get him discharged from the MH so that he could receive the necessary treatment at a private hospital at his own expense.

The medical officer at the station was helpless, as he only had the authority to refer patients to another hospital. The authority for sending any patient back imperatively vested with the higher hospital. After we explained Mrs Venu's plight, the medical officer was kind enough to suggest a solution. He advised Mrs Venu to report sick there, pretending to have a health issue, so that he could refer her to the MH Agra. That way, she could reunite with Venu and spend time together at MH, Agra.

Though she was desperate to meet Venu and was willing to take even that extreme step, we persuaded her to stay with another family until Venu returned. That decision proved wise, as Venu was subsequently transferred from MH Agra to MH Bhopal, 400 kilometres on the other side of Gwalior, because there was no anaesthetist available at MH Agra at that time! Had Mrs Venu reached MH Agra, she would have been stuck there while Venu was transferred to MH Bhopal!

*****

The Yamaha RX-100 bike was highly popular from the mid 80s to the late 90s, and I had cherished the dream of owning one since the day I joined the forces. While posted in Gwalior, I was detailed for a long course at an IAF unit in Delhi, which I saw as the perfect chance to buy my dream bike.

In the defence forces, we could purchase bikes through the Canteen Stores Department (CSD), which offered a reasonable discount. Unfortunately, my favourite bike was not available at the Delhi CSD, so I had to place an order through CSD Meerut.

A week later, I received a call from the dealer informing me that the bike was ready for delivery. Thrilled, I wanted to collect it immediately. However, there was a problem.

At that unit, I only had Sundays off. Since the dealer was closed on Sundays, accepting the bike delivery on that day wasn't an option. Being on a course, taking leave was also out of the question. I felt stuck, unable to find a solution.

My colleague, Goparaju, came to my rescue. He suggested that I take an excused from duty (known as ED) for a day, feigning illness, and quietly go to Meerut to collect the bike. I was unsure if that would work. Sensing my apprehension, he agreed to accompany me.

When my turn came, we confidently walked into the doctor's cabin. The medical officer, who was far senior to us in rank and age, glanced at us with prying eyes, presumably to assess any apparent health issues. A young medical assistant stood by his side, ready to assist with the necessary procedures.

I had not yet decided which illness to feign and was still pondering over it.

"Sir, he needs an ED for a day," I heard Goparaju state bluntly. I expected the doctor to reprimand us for making such a request, as it was entirely at his discretion.

Though he seemed slightly taken aback, he maintained his composure and asked, "Why do you need an ED?"

I was considering feigning some stomach issues, but my friend didn't give me a chance. "Sir, he needs to go to Meerut," he said it straight forward.

I thought it was all over and was fearing the doctor would throw us out.

Surprisingly, the doctor remained calm. "Aren't you aware that you are supposed to be resting in your room while on ED?" he questioned.

"Yes, Sir, but he needs to take delivery of his bike, and we aren't getting any leave from the course. This is our only hope," my colleague daringly blurted out, laying all our worries point-blank.

"Is the situation that bad? By the way, which bike are you buying?" the doctor asked me, a tinge of curiosity evident in his voice.

"Yamaha RX 100," I replied happily that time.

The doctor glanced at his young medical assistant standing beside him, who nodded with an approving smile and remarked "It's a good bike sir, very trendy among the youth."

"'Alright then," said the doctor, approving my ED.

"Sir, I also need ED," my friend persisted.

"Why do you need it? He's going to get it, isn't he?" the doctor asked, somewhat surprised.

"Sir, I want to accompany him. Otherwise, he'll have to ride all alone for such a long distance," Goparaju explained.

Impressed by my friend's straightforwardness, the doctor approved his ED as well.

"Alright, but be careful and drive safely," he cautioned us as we saluted and left his office.

*****

Every soldier was required to undergo an annual medical check-up, with the number of tests increasing with age. Fortunately, my check-ups had always been uneventful. However, on one occasion, my blood tests revealed slightly elevated cholesterol levels. The medical officer promptly issued a warning and advised me to implement *'Lifestyle Modifications.'*

I was referred to a medical specialist to learn about the changes I needed to make in my routine. When I entered the specialist's office, I noticed him extinguishing a used cigarette in the ashtray on his table. The chair struggled to accommodate his large frame, and the buttons of his uniform seemed ready to burst under the strain of his enormous belly.

I sat down on a chair opposite him as he glanced through my medical documents.

"Do you smoke?" he inquired.

"No," I replied quickly, having never felt the temptation to smoke.

"Do you drink often?" He continued, rattling off questions one by one as if reading from a checklist.

"Very occasionally," I answered, recalling how I often saw the doctor at parties, always with a drink in hand, usually staying within arm's reach of the bar counter.

"Stop eating fried foods and avoid oil," he continued his advices.

"I'm not very fond of fried foods and I dislike oil too," I replied honestly.

"Good. Make sure to exercise regularly and find time for a short walk daily," he suggested, readjusting his hefty frame on the chair.

"I'm active in sports and regularly play football or basketball in the evenings," I replied enthusiastically.

"That's great, keep it up. By the way, are you overweight?" he asked next.

I couldn't help but smile at that question. It was the first time someone had asked me if I was overweight. Usually, I faced the embarrassment of being underweight and was quite paranoid about it.

Having narrowly escaped being labelled underweight during my initial medical examination, I always considered gaining a few kilos a monumental task.

And now, here was someone who was clearly well above the overweight limit, asking me if I was overweight! I couldn't suppress a wry smile, which he presumably noticed.

"Everything seems to be okay. Just keep doing what you've been doing," he said, sounding a bit embarrassed as he scribbled something on the paper, presumably to avoid looking at me.

*****

Years later, I had a meeting with another witty doctor known for his ability to connect with patients through humour. I was there for a routine check-up when he noticed that my haemoglobin levels were on the higher side.

"Are you living in the hills? Haemoglobin levels are seen high among those *Pahadi* people," he quipped in his usual style.

"Not exactly in the hills," I shot back, "but on the eighteenth floor of an apartment."

"That hardly matters," he retorted, refusing to let the banter end.

Then I recalled reading that haemoglobin levels tend to be higher among athletes and added, "I run long distances, almost ten kilometres every day."

"I see. Why do you run so much? Do you think it boosts your health?" he responded promptly.

"There's probably no point in doing all that," he continued, supporting his view with an anecdote.

"Let me tell you about a friend of mine, a man in his sixties. He was religious about his morning walks—five, sometimes ten kilometres, rain or shine. One day, as he strolled along his usual route, a speeding truck came out of nowhere and hit him! That was it. All those walks, all that effort, and in the end, it didn't save him."

He leaned back, adjusting his thick glasses, and said with a grin, "See? When your time's up, it's up. All this running and walking—it's just a waste of time, my friend!"

I couldn't help but laugh, despite the dark humour. His point, though debatable, was delivered with such flair that it stayed with me long after the check-up ended.

*****

As part of his duties, Raju—a close friend of mine—was responsible for counselling every personnel in the unit. One day, he was surprised to learn that a lascar named Madan already had three children in quick succession, with a fourth on the way. Concerned, Raju promptly reported this to the Commanding Officer (CO).

The CO, genuinely worried about Madan's well-being, felt that he urgently needed to adopt some form of family planning. After discussing the matter with the Senior Medical Officer (SMO), the doctor suggested that Madan should be counselled to undergo a vasectomy procedure.

A little later, the CO called Raju and instructed, "Ask Madan to report to the SMO. I've briefed him. He'll take care of it."

Raju immediately relayed the message to Madan, who had no idea what it was about. However, being an obedient soldier, he dutifully made his way to the medical centre and registered his name for the sick report—assuming it was some routine medical check-up.

The waiting area was crowded, but after a while, his turn came. Walking into the SMO's cabin, he snapped to attention and saluted smartly. The doctor, sizing him up, asked, "Kya taklif hai?" (What's the problem?)

Madan knew that reporting sick required a valid reason. Thinking quickly, he said, "Sir... khasi aur bukhar hai" (Sir, I have a cough and fever), even adding a few fake coughs to make it convincing.

The doctor conducted a quick examination and reassured him, "It's just seasonal fever. Nothing to worry about. I'm prescribing a cough syrup and paracetamol. Take them twice a day, get complete rest for two days, and you'll be fine."

Madan collected the medicines and returned to his unit. "Sir... mujhse khasi ka dawai diya aur do din ki ED bhi" (Sir, he gave me cough syrup and two days of Excuse Duty), he informed Raju before happily heading home.

Later that evening, during pack-up, the CO called Raju. "The SMO just called me. He said Madan never reported to him. Didn't you tell him to go?"

With a mischievous smile, Raju replied, "Yes, Sir, I did. He went there too. The doctor gave him cough syrup... and two days of Excuse Duty as well!"

HARRY's INN

As part of their official duties, it was imperative for every soldier to visit other bases regularly. Those visits sometimes lasted just a few days, but at other times could stretch into weeks or even months. During such visits, accommodation was typically arranged in the transit rooms within the mess itself.

Back then, without the internet or mobile phones, spending time with friends was the only way we had to pass leisure time. Most of us, except those with pressing commitments back home, loved those short trips. They provided an opportunity to catch up with old buddies and enjoy some time together.

Many bases, which used to be frequently burdened with numerous visitors, often reached full capacity. In such scenarios, usually the mess would arrange accommodation in nearby private hotels. However, everyone preferred staying within the base itself, as it made them feel at home.

It was a standard practice to bump into an old buddy and become his guest for a couple of days. Thankfully, there were plenty of wonderful hosts at every station, who not only provided a place to sleep but also made the stay enjoyable with home-cooked food and a festive time in the evenings!

Many often found shelter with officers whose spouses and children were away on vacation. That arrangement provided some company to those lonely officers as well.

A close friend of mine, Harry was stationed at a busy Air Force base back in those days. He used to have a huge friend circle, which he is still maintaining, and always loved to be in the company of friends.

When his wife was away for nearly a year for the birth of their first child, his house became an extended home for many visitors to the base. During those days, he held a key position and had the luxury of a dedicated cook at home, who was more than eager to try his culinary skills on his master's guests. It made Harry look forward to having guests, as it gave him the opportunity to unwind with wine, jokes, and music during the otherwise dull evenings.

Those who experienced his wonderful hospitality always preferred staying with him on their subsequent visits. Soon, his place earned the popular nickname '*Harry's Inn*'!

Once, an officer arrived at the station for an official task. He had heard about Harry's legendary hospitality and headed straight to Harry's Inn, not even bothering to inquire accommodation in the mess. As always, Harry was delighted to host him.

In the evening, the two friends relaxed on the lawn, unwinding with '*spirited*' drinks in hand. Kishore Kumar's melodies played softly from a stereo, setting the perfect ambiance for the chilly evening. They chatted, sprinkled with a bit of gossip to keep the conversation lively.

Harry's cook remained busy, refilling their glasses and serving up spicy snacks. As the night wore on, Harry suggested they move indoors, not wanting to disturb his neighbours. The guest, still in the mood for more drinks, gave Harry the chance to make up for the past few dry days.

When the conversation lagged, the guest suggested they watch a movie. The TV was in the master bedroom, so they moved the drinks there and continued drinking while watching *Sholay*, an old Hindi movie.

After a while, the guest, apparently exhausted, drifted off to sleep. Ever the considerate host, Harry didn't wake him. His domestic help had long gone, so Harry quietly cleared the room, turned off the lights, and retired to another bedroom.

In the middle of the night, the guest woke up with an urgent need to pee. Half-asleep, he stumbled out of bed, blindly feeling his way through the dark in search of the bathroom door. After some effort, he found a door, opened it, relieved himself quickly, and returned to bed.

Harry got up early in the morning, as usual. He had a habit of going for a morning run. To collect his running gear, he entered the master bedroom, where his guest was sleeping peacefully. Being a good host, he didn't want to disturb his friend and decided not to turn on the light.

As he opened the cupboard, a strong odour filled the air. Confused, he reached for his clothes and found them all completely soaked.

Drawing the curtains slightly, he peered inside the cupboard. With growing horror, he realized that his guest, in his inebriated state, had mistaken its door for that of the bathroom and peed inside.

Blaming himself for not leaving a light on, Harry, ever the gracious host, decided not to embarrass his guest. He quickly emptied the cupboard, loaded the first batch of clothes into the washing machine, and got busy cleaning up the mess.

By the time his orderly arrived, Harry had finished the chores and was setting the last load of clothes to wash.

An hour later, as Harry sat on the veranda sipping tea, his guest emerged in uniform, ready for the day.

"Hey, what happened? Are you not going to the office today?" the guest asked Harry.

"I'm not feeling well—a nasty headache and feeling feverish," replied Harry, keeping his composure.

"Man, you need to improve your drinking stamina. Anyway, I'm here for a few days, and I'll help you with that," his friend jibed as he walked to the gate.

Harry chose not to reply. His gaze lingered on the row of uniforms swaying gently on the lawn's drying line. With a resigned sigh, he picked up the phone and called his boss to inform that he was unwell.

HINDI EXAMS

Official language that the Indian military forces follow is English, though it was common that the verbal communication often switched to Hindi. It was the only way to really connect with the troops, since most of them came from Hindi-speaking regions.

Besides, for those who were unfamiliar with Hindi, social gatherings could feel like being in a comedy show without subtitles. While everyone else laughed at a joke, they would be left trying to figure out what was so funny.

For someone born and brought up in Kerala where the entire communication used to be in Malayalam, speaking Hindi wasn't exactly a breeze either. Most of us only encountered Hindi through those dreaded compulsory exams in school. Sure, we managed to ace the tests. But when it came to actually speaking the language, stringing together even two sentences felt as challenging as scaling Mount Everest!

We've got to give some credit to Doordarshan—the only TV channel back then—for helping us pick up a bit of Hindi. It was the only entertainment we had then! Even though most of the programmes were in Hindi and we barely understood a word, we still tuned in, soaking up whatever we could.

Thanks to all those Hindi-dominated TV shows and programs, we eventually picked up enough to understand most of what was being said. However, speaking even a couple of lines in Hindi still felt like an enormous challenge.

During our initial training, we had a Hindi lecture aimed at improving the language skills of recruits from non-Hindi-speaking states. I still remember how excited we all were before our first class. The seniors had told us that a certain Ms. Lovely would be teaching, with many embellishing tales of her beauty and warning us to be on our best behaviour while attending those classes. Their dramatic build up even convinced a few recruits from the Hindi-speaking belt to attend the non mandatory class.

The next day, we got a real surprise. Ms Lovely turned out to be an elderly lady, just months away from retirement! Her classes were no different from the dull Hindi lessons we had back in school in Kerala. Most of us used the time to catch up on some much-needed sleep. There was a test at the end, which, surprisingly, almost everyone passed—except for a few unlucky ones from Tamil Nadu!

When I arrived at my first field unit in Gwalior, I quickly realized that the only language the local shopkeepers, orderlies, cooks, and waiters spoke was Hindi. Speaking in Hindi, even if it was *'tootee phootee'*, became essential for survival.

The central government offered a voluntary Hindi exam as part of their effort to promote the language, specifically for those from non-Hindi-speaking states. Passing the exam came with a handsome grant, so I applied for it soon after arriving at my first unit and began brushing up on my Hindi grammar—still as confusing as it was back in school.

It wasn't easy, but after burning the midnight oil for several nights, I somehow managed to pass. I was excited, already planning to spend the grant on a new *Yonex Pro* badminton racket.

But instead of the grant, I got the news that I wasn't eligible—because I had studied Hindi in class X! Another attempt to master Hindi and make the most of it had gone completely down the drain!

Hindi exams just didn't seem to let me off the hook. Two years later, during my junior commander's course, I had to face another Hindi test—a five-minute speech in Hindi. Thankfully, we could choose our own topic, so I dug up an old school essay, *'Gai ek paaltu janwar hai...'*, and started practicing it. Unfortunately, a Punjabi friend who loved to poke fun at everyone overheard me rehearsing and spread the word around. Embarrassed at the thought of giving a school-level essay as my talk, I decided to change the topic.

Yet, I didn't want to try my luck on anything too complicated, and pulled out another essay from my school days and confidently spoke on the famous Kerala festival —'*Onam Kerala ka tyohar hai ....* '.

There were rare moments when my Hindi actually earned some appreciation! During a tour, I had a casual conversation with an officer from Punjab. Sensing that he preferred speaking in Hindi, I decided to go with it. We covered a wide range of topics—our home states, crops, festivals, tourist spots, and more. There were times I struggled to find the right Hindi words for some tricky terms, and in those moments, I filled the gaps with Malayalam words. The conversation flowed seamlessly!

"You're speaking Hindi quite well and using words that typically appear only in formal writing. Did you happen to do your schooling up north somewhere?" he asked me before we parted ways.

To be honest, I was stunned when he said that—I initially thought he was pulling my leg. But when he assured me he was serious, I felt a surge of pride. As it turned out, many of the Malayalam words I had substituted fit surprisingly well, purely by chance. With both Hindi and Malayalam sharing roots in Sanskrit, that linguistic overlap had saved me without me even realizing it!

Although I earned some unexpected praise for my Hindi on that occasion, more often than not, it ended up getting me into trouble!

In the nineties, long before the mobile phones became common, the only way to call our residence was through the limited telephone exchange extensions. Since those lines were scarce, they were often shared by setting up parallel connections.

One day at the office, I needed to speak to my wife, so I called her using my extension line. However, another officer's wife, who shared the line, picked up on the first ring. I politely told her I was trying to reach my wife and said I would call back.

When I tried the second time, she picked up again. Thinking she wasn't able to follow what I said, I resorted to explaining the situation in Hindi. Thankfully, that did the trick. The next time I called, she didn't answer, and I was finally able to speak with my wife.

That afternoon, my commanding officer called me into his office to ask about the phone call I'd made earlier. He informed me that the lady I had spoken to felt offended and had reported it to him. He then asked if I had spoken to her in Hindi. When I confirmed, he burst into laughter and advised me never to speak in Hindi with the ladies!

He probably knew how shaky my grasp of conversational Hindi was, particularly with the tricky second-person pronouns—'*Tu*', '*Tum*', and '*Aap*'. Probably, he didn't want any more misunderstandings arising from my linguistic missteps!

While I was posted in Gwalior, my brother came to visit me on his way to Delhi. After a brief stay, I took two days' leave and accompanied him to Delhi. Since he wasn't fluent in Hindi, I saw that as the perfect chance to show off how much I had improved in the language!

Having spent a few months in Delhi on a service training course, I was quite familiar with the area. My brother had a hotel reservation near Connaught Place, which I knew was just a couple of kilometres from the Station.

We decided to take a rickshaw to the hotel, fully aware that the drivers typically quoted inflated fares, especially from the tourists. Negotiating was a standard practice, and eager to put my Hindi skills to good use, I confidently embraced the challenge.

I informed the driver of our destination and asked how much he would charge. *"Sathrah"*, he quickly replied.

I knew fair rickshaw fare for that distance was around twenty five rupees, and felt that the driver was genuinely honest. I turned to my brother and said there was no need of a negotiation.

When we arrived at the hotel, we got out, and I handed him a twenty-rupee note. I waited, expecting him to return three rupees in change. However, from the way he looked at me, I sensed he was expecting something more.

"Bhai saab, teen rupaiye vapis do," I said in my halting Hindi, trying to hide my impatience. (Brother, return three rupees please)

He gave me a mocking look and replied, his irritation evident in his tone, *"Tu Kya bol raha hai? Tum muche pachaas aur do."* (What are you saying? You give me fifty more.)

Noticing the confused look on my face, he probably realized I was a South Indian and hadn't understood him well. He continued in an utterly mocking tone, *"Aare... Satar rupaye ke liye pachas aur dedo... Main sathra nahi, satar bola tha.."*. (Aare... For seventy, give me fifty more.. I had said seventy, not seventeen)

That's when I realized that another number *'satar'* existed in Hindi and it actually meant seventy!

Although my speaking skills had improved, I was still struggling with numbers in Hindi, having only learned up to twenty in school. Clearly, *'satar'* was unfamiliar to me, and I had mistakenly interpreted it as *'sathra'*.

In the end, my brother stepped in, negotiated with the rickshaw driver in his 'pathetic' Hindi, and settled on a fare of fifty rupees!

THE NUMERIC IDENTITY

Numbers often become synonymous with identities. For example, the numbers 7 and 10 are forever linked with football legends Ronaldo and Messi. Similarly, in police stations, constables often have code names which are numbers prefixed with a 'PC', like PC 117. As depicted in movies, even jail inmates are identified by numbers printed on their uniforms, which become their identity while inside.

In the military forces too, numbers hold tremendous significance, often becoming the very identity of a soldier, a unit, or even an address. Just as every post office in India has a unique six-digit PIN code, each military unit is assigned a specific code number for easy identification. Unlike civilian post offices that is fixed at particular location, those units frequently relocate for operational needs, but their designated number remains the same.

As a result, any mail addressed to that unit number will reach its destination without a hitch, whether the unit is stationed in a remote desert along the western border or in the icy cold Kashmir Valley.

When a soldier joins the forces, they are assigned a personal number that becomes their permanent identity. That number stays with them throughout their service, follows them into retirement, and remains with them even beyond the grave.

Every official communication, including posting orders, was issued using those number codes. A single digit change in the unit code could shift the location from a bustling hub like Mumbai to an obscure spot in the North East. It was initially confusing when a posting order arrived, often requiring someone's help to decode the unit numbers. A mistake by that expert could lead to big surprises—turning the joy of being posted to a desirable location into the disappointment of being sent to a remote, undesirable place, or vice versa!

Sometimes, a posting order might show a unit stationed in a metro city, prompting a celebratory moment with friends. But soon after, when you learn that the unit is about to relocate to a remote area, that happiness would evaporate instantly. Unfortunately, there would be no choice but to follow the orders and join the assigned unit!

Various service courses that a soldier undergoes during their career have a course number prefixed with a short abbreviation of the course name. A soldier rarely forgets those course numbers, as they too serve as an identity at times.

We've all encountered situations where two soldiers, upon meeting for the first time, initially act like strangers, offering nothing more than a simple '*Hello.*' But as soon as they start interacting, the first question inevitably concerns their main course number—a detail that immediately establishes their relative seniority and who should be addressed as '*Sir.*' As the conversation progresses, they exchange unit numbers from previous postings and course numbers of other training programs they have attended. When a common number pops up in between, a sense of familiarity begins to grow amongst them. In just a few minutes after having a few common numbers emerged, they would be interacting as if they were buddies for a long time.

When two soldiers meet after many years, they would have forgotten faces and perhaps even names. But those numbers have a way of working their magic, bringing back the good old memories. I experienced it once when I arrived at Ambala with two of my colleagues for an official task.

The mess was crowded, and finding accommodation in the Officers' Mess seemed very unlikely. We approached the manager, requesting a place to stay for a few days. However, since they were expecting an unusually high number of guests, he expressed his helplessness and advised us to contact the Mess Secretary at her residence.

One of my colleagues called the Mess Secretary, a lady officer named '*Bedi*.' She declined our request, citing that we hadn't informed them in advance.

Just then, my eyes caught sight of the nameplate outside her office. The first name seemed familiar. I suddenly realized that she was an officer who had done her basic training with our batch—a course mate!

I called her again, and after a few rings, as expected a female voice answered on the other end.

"Are you sixteen?" I asked eagerly, 16 being her course number.

There was no immediate response—just a moment of dead silence, followed by a surprised "Excuse me?"

In the forces, brevity is essential in communication, but it's equally important that clarity isn't compromised. Clearly, I had failed on that front.

I realized my mistake immediately. Of course, I was referring to her course number, but in the excitement of reconnecting with an old friend, I completely overlooked how it might be interpreted.

She was in her forties, and there I was, asking if she was '*sixteen*'! Looking back on the incident about fifteen years later now with ageing catching up far too fast, I am sure she might have felt a brief moment of happiness then!

I quickly introduced myself, mentioned my course number, and was relieved when she responded with the same enthusiasm you'd expect when catching up with an old friend. After few minutes of friendly talk and explaining our current situation, she cheerfully replied, "How can I refuse to help a course mate?"

Perhaps it was the military camaraderie—or maybe the fleeting thrill of feeling younger—that worked in our favour! Whatever the reason, a simple number worked its magic and provided us with a wonderful shelter in the mess!

TRAIN JOURNEYS

In a country as vast and diverse as India, where military units are stationed from the most remote corners to the bustling cities, trains have long been the lifeline connecting soldiers to their postings, their homes, and everything in between. Even with the rise of affordable and faster air travel, the bonding soldiers share with the Railways remains as strong as ever.

There's something irreplaceable about the rhythmic clatter of the wheels, the camaraderie in crowded compartments, and the slow, scenic journey through India's varied landscapes that continues to captivate every soldier. For many, those journeys became more than just transit—they were moments of reflection, bonding, and the creation of stories that last a lifetime.

With most armed forces units stationed along India's northern, western, and eastern borders, a soldier from the southern regions— especially a Keralite—would inevitably spend a considerable amount of time with the railways. Countless hours would be passed aboard trains, and sometimes even more at intermediate stations, waiting for connecting trains.

The journey to his hometown alone would take three days, with another three required for the return trip. Soldiers who dared to take two vacations in a year would end up spending a significant portion of their leave solely on the journey. And if circumstances demanded additional trips, their time spent on travel would only increase.

As part of his duty, a soldier often needed to travel to other units and locations. If the days spent on such journeys were to be counted, any soldier would have spent a significant portion of his life in a train compartment—watching the scenery rush by through small windows or by observing fellow passengers, enjoying the rhythmic *'tuk-tuk'* music of the wheels moving on the tracks.

Last-minute journeys were the norm for most soldiers, and securing a confirmed reservation was nearly impossible. Yet, in the forces, such challenges were no excuse—soldiers were expected to endure the hardships and reach their destinations on time.

Though a quota was set aside for military personnel, it was like a drop in the ocean compared to the need. Without hesitation, soldiers would prioritize their duty to the nation over personal comfort, often ending up traveling unreserved. During the day, they would squeeze into any available space somewhere, and at night, they would sleep on the floor, with only a sheet or a spread of newspaper beneath them.

The situation was no different when soldiers travelled on leave. Although they could wait for a confirmed reservation—which would inevitably eat into their leave—most chose to take their chances, often embarking without a reservation.

As if the journey wasn't challenging enough, soldiers had to carry considerable luggage both ways. On the way home, it was often *military quota bottles* for waiting friends, or treasures like *Pashmina shawls, Chanderi silk saris*, or a *Kashmiri furniture* for the eager neighbours. The return trip was laden with food—*boiled rice, coconut, chips, banana,* and other Kerala delicacies like '*Achappam*,' '*Kuzhalappam*,' and '*Avalos Unda*.' Those treats brought a comforting taste of home, keeping memories alive until the next leave.

Every soldier is willing to endure such struggles just for spending a well-deserved vacation with their loved ones or for the cause of their country. However, when it comes to traveling with family, things change. He wouldn't dare to travel like he did when he was single. Instead, he would plan everything carefully and make reservations months in advance. If he couldn't book a spot ahead of time, he would use every trick he knew to get it confirmed—sometimes ending up with shady characters and paying a lot more than he should have!

The life of a soldier was full of unpredictable challenges. An unexpected situation across the border could make it necessary for him to report to duty, resulting in the cancellation of a long-awaited leave and shattering all his careful plans. In such moments, the only option was to encourage his family to go on their journey without him, promising that he would join them as soon as the crisis passed.

While it was painful for his loved ones, fauji wives were quick to adapt and understand their fauji husband's commitments. They would often brush off their frustration with a knowing smile, saying, "My husband? Well, you know I'm his second wife... his first love, without a doubt, is the defence forces!"

During those days, while traveling alone on the train, finding ways to pass the time was a challenge. Some chose to lose themselves in a book or catch up on sleep, while others, more social by nature, struck up conversations with fellow passengers and even forged new friendships. And then, of course, there were the chatterboxes—those who dove into endless conversations, covering everything from celebrity gossip to current events, politics, and even cracking jokes to entertain the crowd.

I remember one such journey vividly. It was aboard the Kerala Express, traveling from Gwalior to Kochi. In the same coupe as me was another officer, traveling with his wife. At the time, I had just received my posting orders and was preparing to join a unit in Srinagar in a few weeks. The news from the region was anything but comforting—militancy was rampant, with frequent reports of militant attacks pouring in through the media. Knowing that the officer had just returned from a posting in Srinagar, I figured it was a good opportunity to calm my nerves a little and perhaps get a sense of what awaited me.

The conversation soon turned into a lively discussion, with his wife enthusiastically joining in. She wasted no time in sharing stories from their stint in Srinagar, each one brimming with dramatic flair and plenty of embellishments to keep things interesting. Though she'd only been there for a few months, the way she spun her tales, you'd think she'd lived there her whole life. Soon, other passengers in the coupe gathered around, drawn to her animated storytelling.

One particular tale stood out. She described how militants frequently fired rockets that flew over their quarters, making it sound like they lived in constant peril. According to her, it was nothing short of a miracle that they had survived those dangerous days. Her stories were laced with exaggeration, but her delivery was so captivating that the audience hung on to her every word, eyes wide with admiration. After all, how often do you get to hear first-hand accounts of survival in such harsh circumstances?

As she wrapped up her thrilling narrative, she added, with a knowing smile, that I too would soon be stationed in Srinagar—with my newly married wife, no less.

Suddenly, all eyes were on me, their expressions shifting from curiosity to sympathy. I could practically feel their collective concern, as if they all silently agreed that we were destined to become easy targets for the militants.

Train journeys were often marked by incidents that might not seem amusing at the time, but bring laughter in hindsight. One such story involves a Malayalee friend who was traveling with his newly married wife from Kochi to his duty station in the North. His wife, having only taken short trips before, was understandably nervous during her first long-distance train journey.

When the train reached Nagpur, my friend stepped off to buy some famous '*Nagpur oranges*'. As fate would have it, just as he was returning, the train began to move. Unfazed—having faced similar situations before—he quickly boarded the nearest compartment, intending to walk through the interconnected bogies to reach his wife.

Moments later, as the train continued to roll slowly, he noticed a commotion on the platform. Looking outside, he saw his wife standing there, crying in distress.

Without a second thought, he jumped back onto the platform and ran towards her. In his haste, he tossed the oranges aside, grabbed her hand, and quickly pulled her into the nearest compartment.

Once they were both safely on board, the situation became clear. When the train started moving, she panicked, thinking he hadn't made it back in time and decided to get off. She hadn't realized the compartments were connected and that he could walk through them to reach her.

Had he walked toward the front of the train in search of the fruit seller, he might never have spotted her standing on the platform. Also if the train had picked up speed, the situation could have taken a much more serious turn.

Fortunately, luck was on their side, and what could have been a nerve-wracking ordeal became a light-hearted story they would share for years to come.

These days, with mobile phones in everyone's pocket, it's easy to stay connected and inform someone if anything goes wrong. But back then, it wasn't so simple. If an urgent message needed to be passed to someone on the train, the railway authorities had to intervene—either by physically delivering the message or relaying it over a walkie-talkie to the loco pilot—both of which could only happen at the next station.

A friend of mine – also a Keralite, was once traveling from Delhi to Coimbatore with a few colleagues to attend a training course. For every soldier, such journeys with friends were joyous occasions. They could easily pass time by engaging in interesting conversations or playing cards.

Often, they gulp down a few drinks from the military quota they discreetly carry along. Someone would start to hum a tune, quickly transforming the atmosphere into an impromptu *'Ghazal Night'*!

That evening was no different. The first-class coupe provided the privacy they craved, and drinks and songs flowed freely. Around 10 o'clock at night, the train rolled into Gwalior, where they stocked up on soda and snacks for the long night ahead. Soon, they fell asleep—some sprawled on the berths, others slumped in their seats, empty glasses by their side!

Some time later, the train came to a halt some where. The *'Mallu'* officer — a term affectionately used in the forces for a Malayalee — stirred from his deep slumber, groggy but keenly aware of the urgent need to pee, thanks to the drinks he had indulged in earlier. Wobbling slightly, he made his way toward the toilets, only to find both occupied. Hoping the cool air might clear his head, he opened the compartment door.

Under the soft glow of the moonlight, he could just make out another railway track and a line of bushes beyond it. The stillness and beauty of the scene hinted that the train had halted at the outer signal of a station, waiting for the green light to proceed. The tranquillity of the night and the allure of the landscape captivated him. With a mischievous grin, he thought, "Why not take this opportunity to relieve myself while enjoying the calm and serene nature?"

Acting on impulse, he stepped down from the train, crossed the empty track, and found a secluded spot. Humming an old Malayalam tune, he attended to his business, relishing the calmness of the moment.

But midway through his tune, the night's silence was broken by the distant rumble of an approaching train on the very track he had just crossed. It sped by with a deafening roar, its carriages blurring past. By the time the last bogie had crossed over, he was finished and ready to board back.

Only then did the reality hit him—his train on the other track was gone. The blinking red light at the rear of the train was fading fast, and slowly vanishing into the night.

The desolate surroundings offered no one to call for help. He guessed he was in a forested region of Madhya Pradesh, where the dangers could range from wild animals to roaming dacoits. Yet, thanks to the lingering buzz of alcohol, fear felt like a distant concern.

In the direction where his train had vanished, he caught sight of a faint light in the distance. With no better option, he set off along the tracks, heading toward the distant light.

It was indeed a small, intermediate station, where only local passenger trains made brief stops. The ticket clerk advised him to board the next passenger train to *Bhopal*, from where he could catch a connection to Coimbatore.

A few hours later, he boarded a passenger train and arrived in Bhopal early in the morning. By then, the haze of alcohol had completely lifted. The reality of his situation hit him with full force—he was stranded, his belongings far away on the train he had missed.

With growing concern, he approached the station master and requested to send a message to his colleagues, assuring them of his safety and asking them to retrieve his bags when they disembarked at Coimbatore.

The station master, sensing the urgency, promptly sent the message to the next station, ensuring it would be relayed to the train staff.

The officer then boarded the next available train bound for Coimbatore. However, with no reservation, his only option was to travel in the general compartment, where he found himself squeezed into a corner, sharing a cramped seat with fellow passengers.

The train journey ahead was far from comfortable, with the compartment crowded and the air thick with the hum of conversations. But at least he was on his way.

HEAVEN ON EARTH

Cradled by the towering, snow-capped Himalayas, Srinagar feels like a living masterpiece painted by nature itself. In the spring, the city blossoms into a kaleidoscope of vibrant flowers, while winter transforms it into a pristine wonderland of snow. Its lush gardens, serene lakes, and gently rolling hills weave together to create a landscape totally enchanting. With such ethereal beauty and timeless charm, it's no wonder that Srinagar is lovingly called the '*Heaven on Earth*'.

Just as my marriage was fixed and the formal engagement ceremony was to take place, the Air Headquarters had a surprise in store for me—a honeymoon posting to Srinagar.

The news stirred quite a storm at home, to say the least. While the destination itself felt like stepping into a dream, the reality was far from idyllic. With militancy at its peak, no one even considered visiting the place, let alone staying there for years on duty.

We didn't know how to break the news to the bride's parents, unsure of how they would react. I asked a friend, who was also a relative of my fiancée, to deliver the message. Even he couldn't summon the courage to do it.

On the day of our engagement, her family learned about my posting from their neighbour, whose son was also in the IAF and stationed in Srinagar then. When they arrived for the function that afternoon, their displeasure was evident— partly due to understandable concerns about the location, but mostly because I hadn't informed them personally. By God's grace, everything went smoothly. We got engaged, and a month later, the wedding took place. Soon after, we set off for Srinagar.

Our journey began on the rails, heading north to Jammu Tawi—the northernmost railway station in those days. For nearly three days, we savoured the unique charm and hospitality of Indian Railways, while marvelling at the ever-changing landscapes unfolding through the window.

As we neared our final stop, something magical seemed to happen. A delicate yellow hue began to blend with the browns, with hints of green still lingering, creating a beautiful, almost artistic transition of colours. It was as if nature was putting on a spectacular show for us, making the approach to Jammu and Kashmir feel even more alluring.

When we set foot at Jammu Tawi station, it felt as though we had stepped into a sea of olive green. Soldiers in their army fatigues were everywhere, and the station buzzed with the unmistakable energy of the armed forces.

We could sense the stories in the air—some soldiers, brimming with excitement, were heading home for long-awaited reunions with their loved ones. Others, however, carried the weight of heavy hearts, returning to their units after what must have felt like the briefest of leaves, their cherished time at home gone in the blink of an eye.

There were two ways to reach the enchanting Kashmir valley, each offering a unique experience. Quicker option was a swift flight soaring over the majestic mountain ranges, landing at Srinagar Airport in just half an hour. But for those with a taste for adventure, there was the road—an all-day journey winding through the rugged, hilly roads of the *Pir Panjal* mountain range.

When traveling by road, defence personnel moved exclusively in military convoys. Those convoys, flanked by vigilant armed guards, adhered strictly to security protocols, leaving nothing to chance.

Every soldier reported to a transit camp before their journey, and from that moment, they were considered on duty. They would then be assigned to the next available convoy. If delays occurred—whether due to severe snowfall rendering the roads impassable or heightened militant activity along the route—soldiers would remain safely housed in the camp's transit rooms. Sometimes, that meant spending several days in the camp, waiting for the roads to clear and conditions to normalize.

Each morning, a dedicated mine disposal squad would meticulously scan and sanitize the full stretch of the highway, simultaneously combing from both ends. Only after they cleared it safe for travel, the vehicles could move on the road. Military convoys, always well-protected, travelled under the watchful eyes of heavily armed escorts.

Despite all those stringent precautions, militants would often attempt to infiltrate, disguising themselves as regular travellers. But thanks to the unwavering vigilance of the Indian soldiers guarding the convoy, such attempts rarely could inflict any serious damage.

The journey through the mountains came with its own rewards: breath-taking vistas, towering peaks, and the slow, thrilling anticipation of approaching the valley by land, every turn revealing a new slice of the landscape's untamed beauty.

Far below, the Jhelum River wound its way like a graceful serpent, twisting and turning through the valley as if navigating its own path through the rugged landscape. Along the way, two small camps provided a chance to pause, catch your breath, and soak in the surroundings.

But the true magic starts after crossing the *Jawahar Tunnel* at *Banihal Pass*. On the other side, the mesmerizing beauty of Kashmir unfolded, welcoming you with a vibrant tapestry of colours—nature's own grand display, reminding you why it was known as the Heaven on Earth.

Once a bustling destination teeming with tourists from around the globe, the place was then filled with Indian soldiers in their olive-green fatigues, lining every stretch of the road. Their watchful eyes scanned every vehicle and even the pedestrians walking by, as they performed their duty with unwavering focus—standing on the razor-thin line between life and death.

The threat was real. Militants, blending into the crowd, often concealed weapons beneath the *pheran*, waiting for the opportune moment to strike. Yet, despite their attempts, they rarely stood a chance. The ever-vigilant soldiers, sharp as hawks, would detect danger long before it unfolded, neutralizing the attack before they could make any impact.

Military personnel weren't allowed the freedom to travel outside the camp as they pleased. Using private or public transport was strictly prohibited. Instead, any necessary travel was done in military vehicles, always with armed escorts in tow.

Out of the countless journeys I made during my time there, one stands out in my memory—a road trip to another unit, about sixty kilometres from our camp.

My wife was with me on that trip, and we set off in a Gypsy, accompanied by an armed escort. Halfway through, the Gypsy broke down in the middle of nowhere. Fortunately, luck was on our side as a passing military convoy transporting troops came by. A recovery vehicle towed our Gypsy, and we hitched a ride in the back of a *Shakthiman* truck, packed to the brim with various arms and ammunition. About twenty soldiers sat around us, loaded rifles in hand, eyes scanning the road. For me, it was all in a day's work. But for my wife, it was an adventure she'd never forget—surrounded by armed soldiers on a startling journey through the rugged landscape.

Every season in Kashmir offers a spectacle of its own, each more enchanting than the last. Spring transforms the valley into a vibrant carpet of multi-coloured flowers stretching as far as the eye can see. Come autumn, the landscape undergoes a dramatic makeover as the leaves turn into a rich palette of gold, amber, and fiery red. It's also when the fruit trees were at their fullest, their branches heavy with ripe bounty. The apple orchards, in particular, steal the show—so many plump, red apples dot the trees that they seem to outnumber the leaves themselves!

But as winter creeps in, the valley takes on a more sombre tone, with thick smoke rising from chimneys and casting a dull haze over the surroundings. Yet, when the first snow falls, the magic returns. The entire valley transforms into a pristine winter wonderland, blanketed in pure, shimmering white, like something straight out of a fairy-tale.

Except during the winter months, the weather was usually pleasant, with a gentle chill lingering in the air. None of the quarters had ceiling fans during those days—there was simply no need for them. Winter, however, could be harsh, with temperatures often dipping below zero.

The saving grace was the '*Bukari*'—a type of furnace made from a medium-sized metal drum filled with burning coal. A metal pipe ran from the top to the outside, safely channelling the smoke outdoors.

Lighting up the Bukari was a task in itself, but once it got going, it would burn the coal slowly, radiating warmth for hours.

True, it was a blessing in the winter months, but it was just as dangerous if mishandled. Many people suffered burns when they got too close, desperate for relief from the biting cold. As the coal burned, it produced a colourless and odourless poisonous gas, which normally vented outside through a pipe. But, if the pipe got blocked—often due to neglect in cleaning—the gas could seep into the room undetected. With no smell or colour to warn the occupants, it could render them unconscious in minutes, then quietly taking their lives.

We often heard tragic stories of such deaths in the valley, which made us treat the Bukari with a wary respect, almost like a monster lurking in the corner.

Like other places in the valley, the Air Force base was also beautiful, with nature on full display all around. Back then, the station was filled with apple, almond, and plum trees. The wild apples, plucked fresh from the branches, were far sweeter than any you'd find in a store elsewhere. But as time went on, most of those trees were cut down, since they attracted birds—which, unfortunately, posed a hazard to the flying machines.

Life in Srinagar was an experience unlike any other. We wore our regular summer uniforms until Diwali, which signalled the tipping point for winter's arrival. Soon after, sweaters became a common sight, especially in the evenings.

In the heart of winter, we switched to full winter uniforms, and as temperatures plunged, the heavy '*Coat-Parka*' with woollen pants and a '*Cap-Balaklava*' to shield our heads became essential. Once the first snowfall hit, we added snow boots and leather gloves to our already layered attire, bracing ourselves for the full force of the cold.

Earlier, houses in Srinagar were built with wooden panels to insulate against the biting cold. Later, concrete structures became more common—likely due to a shortage of wood or for added security—though the classic slanted roofs remained so as to prevent snow accumulation.

During Srinagar's prime, many Air Force personnel chose to live in the beautiful city houses on rent. Limited quarters on the base made it necessary, and even in the early days of unrest, there seemed little danger for those in '*blue uniform*,' who enjoyed a vibrant life among civilians.

However, everything changed after a tragic incident in which four Air Force officers were shot by militants while waiting for transport to the base. It was then clear that Air Force personnel were no longer safe living off-base. In response, everyone was moved inside the camp, effecting Srinagar postings into a kind of camp confinement from thereon.

All the essentials for daily life could be found in a small shopping complex at the far end of the campus, which included a provision store, a fruit and vegetable shop, a meat shop, and the must-haves for every fauji: a tailor, a cobbler, and a barber. There was also a STD booth—the lone link to the outside world.

A bit farther from the shopping complex stood another shop affectionately known as the '*Kutte Shop*'—the station's only boutique offering ladies' suits and saris, primarily in traditional Kashmiri styles, along with regional handicrafts and furniture. The name '*Kutte*' had a unique Kerala connection: the shop owner's great-grandfather was a Malayali with the surname '*Kutty*,' which, over time, morphed into '*Kutte*.'

That shop was the go-to spot for the ladies in base, who often browsed its displays for the intricate Kashmiri embroidered suits, though purchases were rare. Nearly every visitor to Srinagar, however, left with at least one beautifully carved item in rich *Akroot* wood, be it furniture or a charming utility piece.

Every day, two Kashmiris in long '*pherans*' would deliver fresh milk to the households, carrying large containers strapped to their bicycles. Due to concerns about militants tampering with supplies, all food items from outside underwent close inspection by security personnel at the entry point. As a precaution, the milk vendors had to take a sip themselves to prove it was safe before distribution.

Essential fruits and vegetables arrived weekly from Chandigarh on a military transport aircraft affectionately known as the '*Sabzi Courier*.' But when the plane couldn't land as scheduled — often due to rough weather — many kitchens were left waiting, hoping for clear skies to bring in their much-needed supplies.

The main camp, known as the cantonment, sat in the heart of Srinagar, about twenty kilometres from the Air Force base and alongside the iconic Dal Lake. That camp housed a military hospital with most specialist services and a small market catering to essential household needs.

At one end of the cantonment was the Air Force Officers' Mess, a charming spot that resembled more like a vibrant garden, filled with a variety of colourful flowers, mostly roses.

Bachelors lived there until rising militant threats made the daily commute to the station far too dangerous.

Winter began settling in soon after Diwali. Having spent the past three winters braving the northern cold, I could adjust quickly. But it was a different story for my wife, who till then had never experienced anything beyond the mild December chill of Kerala. We knew the valley's harsh winter would be a real challenge.

The *'Kutte Shop'* had already stocked up on woollens, and as soon as the temperature started the descent, there was a mad rush for winter clothing. We joined the crowd, stocking up on pullovers, fur coats, gloves, knit caps, and more, bracing ourselves to face our first winter!

As the days went by, temperatures continued to drop further, and the *'Bukharis'* in every home roared to life, sending plumes of smoke into the air. The smoky smell in the neighbourhood reminded me of old steam engine trains running on coal.

We tried lighting ours a few times, but the unsettling stories about that *'monster'* made us cautious, and we soon abandoned it—even as temperatures dipped below zero. Instead, we relied on a small electric blower that barely did the job due to the frequent low voltage, and of course, on the woollens we had wisely stocked up for the season.

One crisp morning in late December, we opened the door to a breath-taking sight: delicate snowflakes drifting from the sky, blanketing everything in a creamy layer of white. Even the leaves on the trees by the fence had donned snowy coats. The front lawn already had a thick six-inch layer of snow. It was our first snowfall—a moment we'd always dreamed of— and we weren't about to let it pass us by. We spent the entire day outside, playing in the snow and even managed to build a cheerful snowman right in front of our quarters.

It was still snowing when we went to bed that night. The next morning, I opened the door, curious to see how things looked.

The snowfall had stopped, but the soft, powdery snow from the previous day had hardened into an icy, slippery layer. Footprints from early walkers dotted the entire length of the road. A gust of wind swept down from the snowy *Pir Pnjal* Mountains, delivering a biting chill that drove me back inside, straight to the warmth of my blanket.

Stepping outside was a real ordeal! First, you had to brave the biting cold, and if you managed that, there was the treacherous road to contend with—snow melting everywhere, leaving the surfaces slick and dangerously slippery. Venturing out meant risking an unexpected, and often embarrassing, fall at any moment.

The power had snapped, rendering the electric room heater useless. A bit later, hunger drove us to munch on a few slices of bread with plain black coffee before quickly retreating under the blanket once again. The fondness we'd felt for the snow barely a day ago had melted away, replaced by curses for the not-so-pleasant aftermath it was causing!

As temperatures dropped to brutal lows, life became truly challenging. Even the water in the pipes leading from the overhead tank to the house would frequently freeze. It was common practice to leave a tap slightly open, allowing a trickle of water to keep flowing to ward off freezing. If the pipes did freeze, the only solution was to heat them by burning paper to thaw the ice and get the water flowing again!

Even the little rats, usually hiding away, would venture out bravely, likely searching for a bit of warmth. Often, they'd sneak onto the bed and nestle quietly behind the blanket.

By March, the snow had melted away, and winter slowly loosened its grip on the land. Tiny shoots emerged from their hibernation, brimming with new life, as the valley transformed into a breath-taking tapestry of vibrant, multi-coloured blooms—a silent yet stunning celebration of nature's renewal.

LIFE IN A CAGE

We had arrived in Srinagar shortly after our wedding. While many newlyweds spent a fortune to honeymoon in such a place, we were lucky enough to experience it as part of a work assignment—earning our pay while living in one of the world's most romantic settings! At least, that's how it seemed. In reality, things were quite different. We spent most of our time confined to the Air Force camp—right when all we wanted was to wander freely, like two lovebirds under the open sky!

Starting our home together meant we needed a lot of household essentials, especially for the kitchen. We picked up a few basics from the local store, and for items like a gas stove, cooker, and kitchenware, we relied on the military CSD canteen. Yet, the list of essentials my wife had made still had some glaring gaps.

Fortunately, a friendly mess waiter, fondly known as *Alibaba*—a local from the valley—helped us procure the rest from the Srinagar market. Before long, we had a functional home, with a kitchen ready to serve a young couple embarking on a new journey.

I kept myself busy with office work, but for my wife, passing the time was a real struggle. Finding a job in the private sector was out of question, given the restrictions on movement we had to follow. Initially, a few visits to Kuttey's shop offered some relief, but the novelty wore off quickly. Being far from home, there weren't any nearby relatives to drop by for a casual visit. As a typical Keralite, she found it difficult to connect with the Hindi-speaking ladies in the neighbourhood, leaving her feeling somewhat isolated. Cooking for just the two of us hardly filled her day. The cable TV, with its limited channels running endless Hindi serials, offered little respite too. For her, the days seemed to stretch endlessly.

Her only comfort was a newspaper that arrived a day late from Jammu, offering a glimpse into the world's happenings, though always a step behind the present. Thankfully, the cold weather invited cosy, long naps, and soon enough, curling up in the warmth of the bed became her preferred way to while away the quiet, chilly days.

When I returned from the office, we often sought comfort in each other's company, passing the time with quiet conversations or sharing glances that spoke volumes about the boredom she was enduring.

On days when the weather was favourable, we'd take a ride, heading to a peaceful corner of the campus where we could lose ourselves in the sight of wildflowers blanketing the fields or gaze at the distant snow-capped mountains. I always carried my Kodak film camera, to capture those delightful moments, though I did it sparingly, mindful of the limited shots each roll could handle.

Just beside our quarters existed a small, untamed forest, home to wild trees and scattered with apple, walnut, almond, and plum trees. An icy stream meandered through that natural sanctuary, making it a favourite spot for picnics and a welcome escape from our routine.

Another place we often frequented was a cluster of small cliffs near the far side of the fence, where we could take in breath-taking views of the Kashmir valley in all its untouched beauty.

Every inch of the valley was a picture-perfect setting for a romantic outing, yet the prevailing situation made such dreams impossible. Leaving the campus without armed escorts was simply out of the question. Still, a few—mostly bachelors—would occasionally slip out on their bikes under some pretext or another. But there was always an uneasy feeling, a sense of unseen eyes tracking your every move, perhaps through the crosshairs of a gun. That lingering uncertainty was enough to dissuade most of us from taking the risk.

Much later, before leaving Srinagar, we did manage to explore its breath-taking landscapes—except for the famed *Shikara* boat ride on Dal Lake, which felt a little too risky to venture into. Yet, none of those moments quite matched the dreamy, filmy scenes one might imagine.

Perhaps whoever managed postings at headquarters didn't have much love for *Mallus*—or maybe they thought posting several of us together would let us create a little Kerala of our own! Whatever the reason, there was a good-sized group from Kerala stationed there at that time, and it was a big relief.

Our otherwise dull weekends turned lively as we gathered at someone's house to lift our spirits. The ladies would get busy gossiping and cooking up some Kerala delicacies, while the men dove into rounds of 56, a card game beloved in Kerala. The two senior-most officers—Nair Sir and Subash Sir, both Wing Commanders at the time—were the obvious choices as team leaders for the two rival teams. As the games progressed and spirits ran high, the rivalry could get heated, with the game sometimes nearly ending in a playful scuffle!

Initially, those gatherings were a weekend affair, but with little else to do, they gradually became almost a daily ritual, bringing us all closer and helping us weather the confined life comfortably.

In a place with far few options for leisure, our gatherings quickly became the talk of the town. The larger North Indian crowd, content with occasional gatherings for formal events, birthdays, wedding anniversaries, and festivals like Diwali and Holi, found it hard to accept that the *Mallus* were regularly enjoying themselves. Leading that subtle disapproval was none other than my boss, who seemed especially put off by our lively get-togethers.

Hoping to join in on the fun, my boss decided to start his own version of those gatherings. Soon, another group formed—my unit, led by our commander—who initiated daily meetups, or, as we liked to call it, an *'informed bouncing.'* He would randomly select one of our homes for those get-togethers, where the assigned host was expected to provide food and drinks. A few party games or an *'Antakshari'* would be squeezed in for entertainment.

As the night wore on, and everyone began to feel it was time to grab some food and head home, the commander would shift gears and launch into stories of his military adventures. As an ace pilot of the Canberra aircraft—a plane famed for its ability to stay in the air for hours—his tales followed suit, stretching on endlessly, as if they might never end!

Everyone stood around, feigning interest and pretending to listen intently, though most were mentally checked out— some even quietly cursing their luck. Faces masked with forced curiosity hid the fatigue and boredom, as no one wanted to risk irritating the boss. If given a choice, they'd have vanished long before, but military protocol demanded that no one leave before the commander. The vintage Canberra would soar high in the sky until the fuel ran low, finally making a quick landing barely a few hours before the dawn. Grabbing the opportunity, the group would disperse in a flash. Not surprisingly, they blamed the *'Mallu gang'*, whom they saw as the root cause of all those misery.

Though mostly dull and boring, those gatherings occasionally offered moments of humour, often at someone's expense. One night, as we gathered at a colleague's house, the Commander was, as usual, in full storytelling mode. The group exchanged looks, hoping to somehow speed up the *'Canberra's landing.'* When the Commander paused to refill his glass, I shifted the attention to a unique decorative piece on the shelf—a finely carved cup made from walnut wood, complete with a wooden screw handle.

One of the wise man among us quickly announced, "That's a walnut crusher!" He explained with a smirk, "You just pop the walnut inside and twist the screw. The shell cracks effortlessly under pressure."

Another officer chipped in, "Did you know the state police use this during interrogations of criminals?"

None of us had ever heard that before, and he continued, "They'd use it by inserting the testicles inside and screw in the handle. The pressure builds pain and makes them spill everything they know."

A mix of shock and amusement spread across the room—some were appalled, while others found it ridiculously funny. Laughter erupted as we joked about that unexpected revelation, lightening the mood and, at least for a while, offering a welcome escape from the Commander's endless stories.

Hearing the spontaneous laughter from the men, the Commander's wife, who had been chatting with the ladies in the next room, came over to see what was going on.

"Hey, Sark... what's the joke? Tell us too, please!" she asked the unit Adjutant, who, as the commander's confidential aide, was close to them. Tactfully he managed the scene and explained the supposed '*real purpose*' of the walnut crusher.

She picked it up, turning it over thoughtfully. "I was looking for one of these! Sark, can you get one for me?" she asked, keeping it back on the stand.

We exchanged glances, everyone fighting to keep straight faces. She examined the crusher one more time and added, "Actually, this one seems a bit small. Sark, see if you can get a larger size."

That was the tipping point—our laughter burst out, unstoppable. She was oblivious to the reason behind it, but the Commander wasn't. He decided to call it a night early. But the poor Adjutant knew he'd certainly bear the brunt the next day. Thankfully, we all were spared form the torturous night adventures for a long time thereafter!

With little else to do on quiet evenings in the confined camp, the bachelors would often '*bounce*' into someone's home, seeking company and a chance to enjoy some home cooked food. We had our share of those impromptu visitors, too.

Two *Mallus*, *Vishy Sir* and *Shyam*, were almost regular visitors, conveniently showing up just as we were about to have dinner. *Shyam*, the ever hungry guest, would cheerfully announce, 'Ma'am, don't bother cooking anything extra; we'll make do with whatever's already prepared!' And, more often than not, my wife and I ended up settling on bananas for dinner on those nights! My subordinate, *Mahendra*— a strict vegetarian from *Karnataka*— often visited with a mission— to savour his favourite *Idli* and *Dosa*. Then there were the more composed ones—*Manesh, Manoj, Rajesh, and Sajeev*— who kept the evenings lively with their endless conversations!

Their presence livened up our evenings and gave my wife a welcome chance to refine her culinary skills.

One evening, we invited a few of the bachelors over for dinner. My wife decided to make a chicken dish using a fowl we'd received as part of the military ration. Though not exactly a seasoned cook, her few past experiments had given her the confidence.

But that chicken was different. Even after cooking it for the usual duration, the meat remained stubbornly tough. She tried again in the pressure cooker for a few more whistles, but despite all her efforts, it was still as hard as rubber. With no other options, we served it to our bachelor guests. They struggled enough with the chicken pieces, but managed to fill their stomachs somehow. As it turned out, my wife's previous experience had been with broiler chicken, and her usual tricks didn't work on the *desi Kashmiri* variety!

Fish curry was always a delicacy for every Keralite. At the camp, we depended on a tiny fish stall at the shopping complex, but they often tried to sell the leftovers from the previous day. Frustrated, we eventually gave up on fish.

My close friend, Menon, a true fish lover, felt the loss even more. Back in Kerala, fish curry was a staple at every meal.

But in Srinagar, he'd given up on his favourite dish due to the lack of fresh options.

Menon's helper, Ramu, lived in his servant quarters and often went to the nearby markets for buying fresh fruits. One day, he spotted a vendor selling fresh fish barely a kilometre from the campus gate. Knowing his master's love for fish, he bought a fresh piece and presented it to Menon. After so many fishless days, Menon finally savoured his favourite dish again.

From then on, Ramu brought fresh fish daily. Menon, not wanting to trouble him every day, even suggested buying in bulk and freezing it, but Ramu insisted it was his pleasure to serve his master.

Things went smoothly until Ramu came down with a viral fever and couldn't leave his bed. For two days, fish disappeared from Menon's menu. On the third day, not wanting to trouble Ramu, Menon decided to find the vendor himself. He asked Ramu for directions, but Ramu, though still unwell, offered to go instead. Menon convinced him to rest a few more days, and set off on his LML Vespa in hunt for fish. Since it was his maiden outing to the city, he asked me to tag along. I agreed, and soon we were riding on his Vespa, enjoying the cool, serene weather on our little adventure. It didn't take us long to spot the vendor at the far corner of the tiny market.

The setup was unmissable—not just for the neatly displayed fish on a polythene sheet but for the striking appearance of the seller: a Kashmiri girl in her twenties, as radiant as a fresh red apple, sitting on a low wooden stool and dressed in a bright red traditional pheran. It took us just a second to understand why Ramu had been so enthusiastic about buying fish every day!

Ever since that incident, the talk of the town was that Menon had dismissed his domestic help and taken on the daily fish-buying duty himself!

SNOWY MOUNTAINS BECKON

Winter in the valley reached its peak in January, with temperatures frequently dipping below the freezing point. The melting snow, coupled with biting winds sweeping down from the snow-capped mountains, made the cold all the more unforgiving.

I had read that in the Arctic region, animals enter hibernation, slowing their bodily functions to conserve energy. It helps them to adapt to the brutal winter months and survive. It seemed my wife had perfected a similar art— spending most of her time nestled under a thick blanket, drifting in and out of sleep to escape the relentless chill.

While we were braving the unforgiving winter in Srinagar, I received an order for a temporary attachment to another unit. At first, the idea of escaping the biting cold brought a wave of relief. That relief, however, was short lived when I realised my destination was a remote unit, nestled deep within the *Ladakh* mountain range, near the Indo-Chinese border.

The place was notorious for its merciless winters, where temperatures rarely rose above single digits, even in the so called milder months. The very thought of enduring temperatures a further 20 degrees lower sent shivers down my spine well before I even set foot there.

The unit was an IAF airfield nestled amidst towering, snow-clad mountains. It served as the lifeline for troops stationed in the surrounding mountain ranges and at remote border outposts. During winter, when all roads to the *Ladakh* region became impassable, military aircraft provided the sole link to those isolated areas.

Whenever the need for additional manpower arose in the region, it was standard practice to temporarily assign personnel from other units. I assumed my attachment was just one of those routine reinforcements.

The station had a reputation as a kind of *'correction centre'*—its remote location and punishing conditions were considered perfect for straightening out the troublemakers. I'd heard such stories before, so when I received news of my attachment there, I couldn't help but mentally retrace my recent actions, wondering if I'd done something to warrant that particular assignment.

Eager to know how long the attachment would last, I reached out to a colleague in Delhi. While he couldn't provide an exact duration, he advised me to prepare for at least a month or two. Worried about leaving my wife behind in a place she was already finding difficult to adjust to, I began considering alternatives.

One option seemed promising: taking her to Chandigarh, the main hub for flights to my destination. With its pleasant weather and lively city atmosphere, I felt Chandigarh would be a far more comfortable place for her to stay. Besides, since military aircraft operated regularly between Chandigarh and my destination, I could easily visit her—perhaps on weekends, if not more often.

I had a few friends in Chandigarh and with their help I managed an accommodation for her in the Officers' Mess. After settling down and enjoying the weekend with my wife, I boarded a flight to my destination on Monday morning. The weather was rough there, and the plane couldn't land, forcing us to return to Chandigarh. It was a very common occurrence in winter, as the mountain weather was deceptive and could shift drastically in a matter of minutes. Even the following day brought no improvement, and the aircraft couldn't go.

It felt like a blessing in disguise, as it gave me a few extra days to spend with my dear wife in that beautiful city. Finally, on the third day, the skies cleared, and I was back on the plane, ready for my adventure among the snowy mountains.

Whenever an aircraft landed there, nearly everyone at the station would gather on the tarmac to receive it. It wasn't a family station, so most of those stationed there kept their families in Chandigarh, allowing them a sense of closeness and the chance to visit whenever their schedules permitted. Often, wives would send home-cooked meals for their husbands with the aircraft crew. A few others, who couldn't go long without trendy treats like burgers, pastries, fried chicken, and pizzas, relied on those flights to bring their favourites from the city.

Naturally, many showed up at the tarmac to claim those special deliveries. For others, the gathering was a rare chance to refresh their eyes, tired from endless views of snow, with a refreshing sight of new faces and enjoy a break from the monotony of routine.

The day I landed, it was no different—nearly the entire station, including the commander had gathered on the tarmac, braving the icy, bone-chilling weather. I introduced myself to the commander, who promptly advised me to take complete rest for two days to acclimatize to the new environment.

In high-altitude areas, where the air is thinner and oxygen levels were significantly lower, the lungs needed time to adjust. Skipping the adaptation period could lead to adverse effects, from breathing difficulties to even seizures.

The view of the snow-covered mountains was breath-taking— a vast, pristine expanse of white stretching endlessly in every direction. I felt like a tiny ant trapped in a giant bowl of snow, with nothing but whiteness surrounding me.

It reminded me of a psychometric test during my SSB interview, where random images would be flashed on the screen, and we had three minutes to weave a story around it. At one point, they showed a blank white screen and asked us to create a story from that empty canvas. Lacking any spark of creativity, I wrote, *'Life without all the colours is dull and boring.'* Standing there, surrounded by icy white walls, I truly felt the weight of those words.

After taking in the serene view for a while, I headed to the Officers' Mess with a few others who had flown in with me. I was bundled up in layers designed for that extreme cold—woollen trousers, a pullover, a thick coat-parka for extra warmth, a balaclava cap to cover my head, along with leather gloves and snow boots. Altogether, the entire gear weighed at least fifteen kilos, and I knew I'd be carrying that extra weight the entire time I was there.

Despite all that protection, I could still feel a biting chill seeping through. After a quick lunch, I walked around a bit, taking in the snow-laden views. Within minutes, my eyes grew tired of the glare from the endless white, and I quickly slipped inside the room arranged for my stay.

The *bukari* used there was a different kind—one that ran on kerosene instead of coal. The room boy lit it and explained how it worked. A kerosene tank was placed at a height, and when the tap at the bottom of the tank was opened, kerosene would flow drop by drop into the *bukari*, which could then be lit with a matchstick.

Handling was certainly easier than the coal *bukari*. Plus, there was no risk of poisonous gas leaking out and silently endangering the occupants.

However, if the flame accidentally went out, kerosene would continue to drip, gradually spreading across the carpet on the floor, and thereafter even a tiny spark could trigger a catastrophic fire.

After explaining the operation, he reminded me, "Sir, better to close the tap and put it off before you go to sleep".

The fact was, both types of bukaris—coal and kerosene-powered—came with their own risks. Yet, many still dared to leave them running through the night.

The reasoning was simple: they'd rather face that risk than suffer the bone-chilling cold. Perhaps, for most, the warmth was worth the gamble.

The clothes in my suitcase were as cold as ice, and I had no desire to change out of the uniform I was wearing. Slowly, the warmth from the bukari began to spread through the room.

I wanted to speak to my wife, and the only way to reach her was through the Air Force exchange. I called and booked a call to Chandigarh, then lay down, hoping to catch a bit of sleep. But the room boy's warning kept echoing in my mind. I glanced over at the bukari, and decided it might be wiser to stay awake.

Around four in the evening, the room boy arrived with a large tea container. He poured a steaming cup of tea and placed it on the wooden board beside me. Then he filled a flask with extra tea and set it aside. Perhaps he thought a little more tea might cheer up my spirits.

"Shall I bring your dinner to the room?" he asked sympathetically.

Though the offer was considerate, I was already feeling restless and decided it would be better to step out of the room and see a few fellow humans in the dining hall. I thanked him and declined his offer.

Halfway through my second cup of tea, the exchange patched me through to my wife in Chandigarh. Her voice crackled and warped, sounding as if it came from the far reaches of the outer space. The volume swung unpredictably, sometimes fading and sometimes echoing. The culprit was undoubtedly the aging tropo communication network, apparently limping along in the harsh weather. But none of that mattered. I was just grateful to hear her voice, and she seemed equally delighted.

For the next hour and a half, I found myself practically shouting into the phone, often repeating sentences to ensure she could hear and understand what I said. Despite all the struggle, that call was an absolute delight—a much-needed reprieve from the overwhelming loneliness I had been feeling.

After dinner, I lingered in the dining hall, captivated by the chilling tales shared by a few colleagues stationed there. Their stories painted vivid pictures of the harsh realities of life in that frozen outpost. But as the clock neared half past nine, they all quickly retreated to their rooms, and I hesitantly followed suit.

I had learned earlier that the station operated on captive power—electricity generated on-site using diesel generators. To conserve fuel, the power supply to all non-essential services used to be shut off from ten at night to five in the morning. Sleep was nowhere near, and I wasn't keen on curling up under the icy cold blanket so early. However, the thought of spending the night in a room slowly losing its warmth nudged me into action.

The bukari—the fire-breathing monster—needed to be lit and extinguished before the power cut. Reluctantly, I returned to the confines of my tiny room, bracing myself for my first night in the icy embrace of Ladakh.

Since I was still in the mandatory acclimatization period, I spent most of the next day cooped up in my room. The only breaks from the monotony came during brief trips to the dining hall, where I caught up with fellow officers—a welcome respite from the slow, seemingly endless pace of life.

Feeling restless, I found myself troubling the exchange a few times, calling my wife even though the voice clarity was still at the mercy of the weather gods. Our conversations were mostly one-sided, with her filling the silences while I listened. I didn't have much to share—my contributions were limited to a repetitive cycle of snow, cold, food, and sleep!

By the time I was ready to get on with my assigned task after the acclimatization period, the weekend had arrived. Knowing that no official tasks were likely to happen during the holidays, I thought of making a quick trip to Chandigarh. I even secured permission from the Commander. However, the nature seemed to have other plans. No aircraft could land due to unfavourable conditions, and I found myself stuck in the same monotonous routine for two more days!

I wanted to call my parents in Kerala. But, public telephone facilities were non-existent at the station. Someone mentioned that an STD facility was available at an Army unit about three miles away. It was a temporary arrangement by the military to facilitate the troops to contact their dear ones, by interconnecting a few Army units through cables that snaked across the hills and eventually connected to a distant P&T exchange.

However, he warned me that the line mostly remained out of order—courtesy of foxes and other wild animals that seemed to have a peculiar fascination for breaking the wires that crossed their territory.

With nothing to occupy me during the dull weekend, I decided to try my luck and see if I could call home. On Saturday morning, after breakfast, I set out on the snow clad road toward the Army unit that had the STD phone facility, accompanied by the room boy, who knew the route well.

As I trudged through the melting snow, weighed down by heavy winter gear, I felt the sting of the thin air. Each step left me puffing and breathing hard, forcing me to slow down and pause occasionally to keep my breathing steady. After an hour of relentless struggle through the snow, we finally arrived at the Army unit —only to find the phone silent and useless, just as I had feared.

Disheartened, we retraced our steps back to the base, the weight of disappointment heavier than the trek itself.

Life for every soldier in such places was incredibly challenging—both physically and mentally. On one hand, they had to endure the biting cold and the thin, oxygen-deprived air, which pushed their physical resilience to its limits. On the other, they grappled with the psychological toll of monotony, surrounded by an endless expanse of glaring white snow.

The only splash of colour amidst that stark landscape came from military vehicles—Olive Green for the Army and Dark Royal Blue for the Air Force. Without them, the entire world around them could have passed for a scene from an old black-and-white photograph.

Everyone eagerly awaited their turn for leave—a chance to be with the loved ones and escape the hostile weather and haunting whiteness. But leaving wasn't simple. Soldiers had two options: endure long, treacherous journeys on Army vehicles along the perilous mountain roads that often took days, depending on weather and road conditions, or board a military aircraft for a quicker passage to the mainland.

During the winter months, when the roads were closed, everyone relied entirely on the military aircraft—a lifeline in the otherwise isolated and unforgiving environment. Naturally, that led to long queues of hopefuls, each eager to secure a spot on the flight alongside the tons of load it carried.

Once aboard, a collective sigh of relief would spread among the soldiers. They knew they were in the safe hands of the Indian Air Force pilots—thorough professionals who navigated the treacherous terrain with the skill and familiarity of native birds. However, the journey was far from a commercial flight experience - no frills, no plush seats, and certainly no air hostesses serving tea and snacks.

The faces of the soldiers reflected none of the hardships they had endured over the past few months. Instead, there was a palpable sense of pride and a rekindled energy. A long-absent grin would slowly spread across their lips, reflecting the relief and anticipation of reuniting with loved ones and escaping the biting cold, though only for a while.

The aircraft would naturally be loaded to the brim, carrying the maximum number of passengers within the permissible safety margins. During the winter months, it was relatively easier to secure a seat, as the cold temperatures allowed the aircraft to handle heavier loads.

In summer, as temperatures rose, the already thin air at such high altitudes became even less dense, drastically reducing the aircraft's lift capacity. That meant planes could only take off with significantly lighter loads on outbound flights.

As a result, only emergency cases were prioritized, leaving the rest of the troops with no choice but to endure long, gruelling journeys by road in army convoys to reach the mainland. Ironically, it made most of the troops love the harsh winter months a bit more than the relatively comfortable summer months.

On Monday, the commander assigned me the task of studying and preparing a report on a specific operational subject. It was well within my expertise, but I immediately realized the assignment was futile. The proposed task was utterly impractical at that station, something anyone familiar with the place would understand.

Nevertheless, I quickly studied the subject and had my report ready in just a couple of days. Honestly, I was baffled as to why I was being given such a pointless job.

However, when I submitted the report, the commander returned it, asking me to explore further possibilities for achieving a positive outcome. I had already outlined, in detail, why the task wasn't feasible, but my explanations seemed to have fallen on deaf ears.

A few days later, I resubmitted the report with additional clarity, emphasizing the impracticality of the proposal. But the commander wasn't ready to relent, and my report came back to me like a boomerang.

For the next three weeks, the file kept moving back and forth. I submitted the report multiple times, each time with more detailed justifications, only to have it returned with instructions to revise it.

Sensing something amiss, I called my unit commander in Srinagar and explained the situation in detail. That night, I received a directive to meet the commander the following day and submit the report again.

The next morning, as instructed, I met with the commander and handed over my report. He accepted it, took a customary glance through the pages, and asked, with a hint of curiosity in his voice, "Who was originally supposed to report here?"

My discussion with a colleague in Delhi had shed light on the situation, and I told him the name. The commander's expression shifted, and there was a tinge of regret in his voice as he said, "Oh! That is sad. If it wasn't you, what are you doing here? You can leave immediately."

His words were like music to my ears. I was finally cleared to leave the station, away from the brutal weather and the solitude I had endured.

As it turned out, someone else had originally been slated to report there. However, when that officer couldn't make it for some reason, HQ sent me as a backup without informing the commander about the change. Till I explained, he had mistakenly assumed I was the one slated for the 'task'.

In hindsight, while the mix-up was frustrating, it gave me a unique and challenging opportunity to experience the unforgiving isolation at a place nestled among the Siachen Glaciers in all its true and horrifying '*avatar*'.

In my hurry to reach Chandigarh and be with my wife for her birthday the next day—her very first after our marriage—I quickly got ready to board the next available aircraft. But fate had other plans.

A heavy snowfall that had started the previous night had draped the entire landscape in a thick, white blanket, making the chances of an aircraft arriving almost impossible.

As I wandered near the tarmac, uncertain and restless, a colleague approached me. "One of our helicopters is heading to *Jammu*. You may board it and reach *Jammu* by evening, then catch a train from there to Chandigarh" he suggested.

Without hesitation, I seized the opportunity. By noon, we landed in *Leh*, where we needed to refuel before continuing onward. But luck wasn't on my side. The weather worsened, forcing a night halt there.

The next morning, I kept my eyes fixed on the sky, hoping for a break in the weather. It improved slightly, but still wasn't ideal for the helicopter to take off.

Then, from the southern sky, I heard the familiar roar of a jet. My heart leaped with hope, only to sink moments later when I realized it was the Indian Airlines flight from Jammu. With it's on board Instrument Landing System, it could land effortlessly, even in those harsh conditions.

Just then, I noticed a young officer hurriedly making his way to board the flight. Curious, I struck up a conversation. He, too, was desperate to reach Chandigarh that very day—to be with his fiancée on her birthday. When I told him I had the same urgency, he yelled, "Let's go!"

I had neither a ticket nor the proper civilian attire for the private air travel. But at that moment, none of it mattered. Thanks to the enthusiastic colleagues and the IAF controlled ATC, I managed to secure a last-minute ticket, and within fifteen minutes, we were on board the waiting aircraft! Fellow passengers stole curious glances at me, likely amused by the heavy military winter gear I was wearing, which probably gave the impression that I had just stepped off a battlefield!

Thirty minutes later, we landed in Jammu and immediately boarded a train to Chandigarh. By the time I reached the guest house, only a few precious hours remained of that beautiful January 31st evening. I hadn't informed my wife of my last-minute plans, unsure whether I would even make it.

When she opened the door, her eyes widened in astonishment. "You made it!" she whispered, still in disbelief.

I hugged her, yelling "Happy Birthday!" then reached into my pocket and presented my first ever birthday gift to her—'*The Leh-Jammu Flight Ticket!*'

ON THE WAR FRONT

The day my wife returned to Srinagar with our firstborn was far from ordinary. It coincided with the discovery of Pakistani intruders on a mountain peak in the *Drass* sector in J&K—an incident that would soon escalate into a full-scale military conflict with our neighbours.

Soon, everyone in uniform was called into action, with many of us spending long hours—often day and night—in the office, preparing for the inevitable. Those on leave were recalled, and additional forces began arriving at our base. I, too, had no choice but to join my duties after quickly settling my family into the comfort of our military quarters.

At home in Kochi, my wife had the support of many, helping her with every need as she adjusted to the demanding life with our new-born. But in Srinagar, things were different. The sole helping hand she had expected from me, while settling into our new role as young parents, also disappeared. She had to navigate the challenges of motherhood all alone. Despite the difficulties, she quickly adapted, finding rhythm in her tiny world in the valley.

Day by day, the situation grew tenser. Srinagar, located close to *Kargil* - the main battlefield, became the epicentre for air operations. Though it had not yet escalated into full-scale war, constant attacks and counterattacks were underway. The Indian military was on high alert, prepared for any eventuality, though no one knew when the order to strike would come. The atmosphere was charged, with a feeling that anything could happen at any moment.

Once the Air Force jets began targeting enemy intruders and their camps in the *Kargil* sector, we knew there was a high likelihood of a counterattack from the Pakistani military. If that happened, our base would undoubtedly be one of the first targets to face enemy air attacks. The tension was palpable, and the uncertainty weighed heavily on everyone.

The local administration had also taken steps in preparation for a potential enemy intrusion. There were deep culverts in front of every quarter, originally constructed as drains for melted snow and rainwater. However, their another critical purpose was to function as trenches, providing some level of protection from the blast effects of bombs and missiles in the event of an attack.

The nights were spent in total darkness or, at best, with only the bare minimum lighting. Windows in offices and houses were covered with thick black paper to prevent even the faintest sliver of light from escaping. Every stretch of road inside the campus remained shrouded in darkness, with all streetlights switched off. Vehicles moving along the roads adopted blackout measures, their headlights and tail lights covered with filters to dim their glow. Those precautions were essential to prevent enemy aircraft from visually spotting the camp under the cover of night.

As the situation escalated, security vehicles began making regular rounds through the camp, urging all families to follow safety precautions diligently. They were instructed to take shelter in the trenches as soon as they heard the air raid siren. They had to even undergo a few practices too. Those heightened precautionary measures stirred up the families, and they concluded that the once distant threat was now a very real and certain danger.

The sudden turn of events left everyone deeply shaken, prompting most of them to stay within the relative comfort of their homes. On the rare occasions when they ventured out and crossed paths, their conversations inevitably centred on the tensed situation unfolding around them. Rumours spread like wildfire during those brief meetings, fuelling anxiety even further.

The situation worsened when the camp's only STD booth—soldiers' sole link to their families back home—went out of service for a few days. Anxiety peaked when whispers emerged that the exchange had been deliberately shut down in preparation for a war. With no calls going through, dear ones back home had to depend what came on the media and they grew increasingly concerned for the safety of their soldier sons and family in the battlefield.

Soon, another piece of news began doing the rounds—a plan to evacuate families to safer locations in the mainland, with arrangements to send them onward to their hometowns. That news stirred unease among the families. None of them wanted to leave their *fauji* spouses behind. Being in the camp, however tense, meant they could catch occasional glimpses of their loved ones. Once evacuated, they feared they would be left in the dark, without any first hand updates from them.

The administration, in fact, had a contingency plan in place to minimize civilian casualties if the conflict escalated into a full-scale war. Fortunately, the plan was never put into action, sparing everyone the added emotional turmoil it would have caused.

Wounded soldiers from the warfront were regularly airlifted to the Srinagar Air Force base by military helicopters. The station's medical team sprang into action the moment they arrived, providing immediate care and preparing them for further evacuation. Once stabilized, they were swiftly transferred onto military transport aircraft and flown to other major cities, where super-specialty hospitals awaited to provide the advanced treatment they urgently needed.

Amidst all that, the station also bore a deeply heart-wrenching responsibility—receiving the coffins of brave soldiers who had made the ultimate sacrifice for the country. Each arrival was met with solemn homage before the mortal remains were sent onward to their hometowns for performing the final rites.

As the conflict intensified, the number of casualties surged, and with it, the number of coffins arrived at the station too. The sight of those draped in the tricolour became a heart-breaking, yet constant reminder of the steep price paid in the name of valour and duty.

"You never know what tomorrow might bring. Be prepared," our commander had advised as we geared up for action. He stressed the importance of keeping personal records—such as wills and nomination papers—updated to avoid any complications in case of an unfortunate event.

"I'm sure, like in my case, your spouses don't have a clear understanding of your financial matters," he continued.

"I suggest you write down your investment and bank details clearly and store them somewhere safe. If anything were to happen, your spouse shouldn't be left searching in the dark."

At the time, we didn't take his words too seriously. But then, an unfortunate event occurred that shook us all, and we realised what those warnings meant.

A few days into the conflict, a helicopter from our base was shot down by enemy forces during a mission, tragically claiming the lives of all four crew members on board. The news struck us like a thunderbolt, leaving us shaken.

That very morning, we had seen their faces—filled with life, purpose, and determination as they prepared for their mission. And then, in the blink of an eye, they were gone—reduced to memories. It was a haunting reminder of life's fragility, especially in the unforgiving shadow of war.

True, we couldn't compare ourselves to those on the war front, fighting face to face with the enemy. They fought with unwavering courage, while we lived under constant threat. The thought that a single bomb could turn us into mere memories never left our minds. Our fight was to prevent it while continuously supporting those at the war front.

The Indian military fought with unyielding grit, their resolve as steadfast as the unforgiving terrain they battled on. The adversaries stood no chance against the sheer courage and determination of the Indian soldiers, who pressed forward despite relentless challenges. As the indomitable spirit of our forces surged, the enemy's resistance began to unravel. Some fled in desperation, while those who dared to stand their ground were swiftly and decisively overpowered.

In due course, the Indian military triumphantly recaptured every mountain range that the enemy soldiers had crept into. The tricolour once again fluttered proudly over the peaks, a stirring symbol of the courage, resilience, and ultimate sacrifice of our brave soldiers.

The tension in the air was palpable, with the constant threat of a full-scale war hanging like a dark cloud overhead. Late nights and early mornings were often shattered by the blare of warning sirens, sending everyone into immediate action. By then, it had become second nature—lights would be snuffed out in an instant, and we'd race to the nearest trenches, moving with the urgency of a well-rehearsed drill. It was a ritual we had all come to know too well, a rhythm of survival that we had grown numb to, yet one that kept us on edge, always alert, always ready.

The battle had ended, and operational efforts to the war zone reduced drastically. However, we feared that the sting of defeat could provoke the enemy to resort to other tactics in their arsenal, seeking revenge for their humiliation. That forced us to remain on high alert for a few more months. Yet, having faced such a crushing loss, the enemy never mustered the courage to strike again.

After several months, a sense of normalcy slowly returned. Gradually, we eased back into our routine tasks, carrying the resilience forged during those challenging days while leaving the scars of battle behind.

My son was only three months old when the conflict began, and by the time it ended, he was already crawling! He, too, had his own brush with the chaos—huddling in the safety of the trenches, clinging to his mother whenever the air raid sirens blared. He was probably the youngest to be caught in the heart of all those military actions there!

THE DETECTIVE

Unlike most other professions, the responsibilities of a military officer are seldom limited to a single role. Beyond the duties for which they are enlisted, each officer is expected to oversee a diverse array of tasks, including administration, human resources, finance, security, and more. While specialists handle these functions at higher levels, at the unit level, the responsibility often falls on the available officers.

Besides, there are other responsibilities referred to as '*secondary duties*,' which are critical for the smooth functioning of the unit. These include managing non-public fund ventures such as CSD outlets, gas agencies, and local military schools, as well as overseeing resources and infrastructure for sports, security, and personnel welfare.

Officers may also need to take on various mess-related roles, such as the President, Secretary, or the Food Member in the Mess Committee. Those duties complement primary roles rather than replace them, often requiring additional time and effort that extends well beyond standard working hours.

In addition, officers are regularly called upon to fulfil many other interim responsibilities. For instance, they might serve on Boards of Officers to conduct studies on matters such as installing surveillance systems or constructing housing quarters. They also need to conduct Courts of Inquiry (CoI), which investigate issues ranging from minor accidents to major air crashes, or from breaches of discipline to severe cases like rape or murder.

The dynamic and demanding nature of these responsibilities underscores the unique adaptability and commitment expected from a military officer, often requiring them to wear many hats simultaneously, with little room for error.

Years ago, while I was serving in the northern sector, a tragic incident unfolded on a Diwali night.

Sepoy Kumar, a guard stationed at an isolated post of the station, was found dead at his post. The other two guards on duty with him, Sepoy Ramesh and Sepoy Basappa, claimed it was a case of suicide.

As is customary in such cases, the civil police were called in to investigate. However, their findings did not support the suicide theory. Suspicion of foul play arose, and during questioning, it was revealed that a few others had also visited the post that night.

Suspicious of their involvement, the police detained Ramesh, Basappa, and five others who had visited the post that night for further interrogation. Despite extensive questioning, they were unable to make any breakthrough.

Eventually, the case was handed over to the IAF, and the witnesses were placed in military custody. A Court of Inquiry was convened to investigate the incident, and I, along with another officer, was assigned to conduct the inquiry.

Growing up, I was fascinated by detective novels, with fictional sleuths like *Hercule Poirot* and *Sherlock Holmes* capturing my imagination during the teenage years. For fun, a close friend and I even started a 'detective agency' and ambitiously named it Scotland Yard.

Unsurprisingly, no one ever approached us with real cases! Instead, we kept ourselves entertained by 'investigating' trivial mysteries, such as the theft of bananas and toddy from the backyard, the poisoning of a neighbour's dog, and the case of a local girl who ran away with her boyfriend. Needless to say, none of those cases ever reached a conclusion.

Years later, when I was tasked with investigating a real murder case, the long-dormant detective in me sprang to life. It felt like the perfect opportunity to put my long-imagined sleuthing skills to the test.

My team member and I met with the civil police officers involved in that case to gather insights. The guard had sustained a fatal bullet wound to the chest. While the police began their investigation treating it as a suicide—based on the statements of the other two guards—circumstantial evidence suggested otherwise.

During the interrogations, the prime witnesses—Ramesh and Basappa—began shifting blame onto one another, deepening the layers of suspicion. It also became evident that someone had deliberately attempted to erase all traces of evidence from the scene, further complicating the investigation.

One of the biggest challenges I faced during the investigation was my lack of fluency in Hindi. The guards primarily spoke a rustic, native dialect of Hindi, while I, being a Keralite, was barely proficient in the language. My previous attempts to converse in Hindi often ended in laughter among my friends, highlighting how inadequate my skills were. I knew it wouldn't suffice for a serious investigation.

Fortunately, an interpreter-cum-translator was assigned to our team to bridge the language gap. However, it didn't take long to realize that he was more of a hindrance than a help. His involvement often slowed the process and diluted the interrogation's impact. I found that dealing directly with the guards in my broken Hindi, despite the occasional missteps, was far more effective. Nevertheless, we continued to rely on him for translating documents and filing the proceedings accurately.

We began the investigation by questioning the guards about the details we already knew, intending to gradually build on their responses. However, they simply repeated what they had told the police. Two days passed with no progress, and the initial enthusiasm of our team began to wane.

Despite employing every tactic we could think of, their responses remained rigid and mechanical—clearly rehearsed from countless prior interrogations. No matter how we approached them, we found ourselves trapped in a frustrating loop, going in circles and making no real progress.

It was as if we were chasing shadows, stuck at the very point where we had begun.

That's when the detective stories I had devoured in my younger days sparked an idea. Drawing inspiration from those brilliant fictional sleuths, we decided to switch tactics—approaching the investigation from an entirely new angle.

Every great detective knows that the key to solving a case often lies in uncovering the motive. After all, every crime is driven by a reason—it's hard to imagine someone killing another purely for fun. For some, the motive might be as trivial as teasing or seeking revenge, while for others, it could involve a substantial reward or gain. I believed there had to be a similar driving force behind that case.

Soldiers performing monotonous duties in far remote places, away from their family, undergoes immense pressure. Under such circumstances, even a minor issue can ignite their darker impulses. That is precisely why the forces emphasize periodic counselling sessions, providing a space for personnel to voice their concerns and relieve pent-up frustrations.

In that case, however, we began to suspect that such measures might have been overlooked, potentially allowing unresolved tensions to fester.

There was no doubt that it was a case of murder. An outsider would have had to pass multiple guard posts to reach that remote location, which would undoubtedly have attracted attention. The only individuals known to have visited the post were the supervisor and his team, who arrived only after the crime had occurred.

That narrowed the possibilities to two scenarios—either one of the two guards at the post was responsible, or they had conspired together to commit the crime. But there they were, accusing each other of being the perpetrator.

We interrogated every witnesses again, primarily focusing on their activities and interactions in the days leading up to the incident.

To our surprise, neither seemed to know much about the deceased—not even basic details about his family or children—despite having served together for over a year. It became apparent that the victim might have been a solitary figure, someone who preferred to remain aloof and avoided building close relationships with his peers.

During our questioning, another Sepoy who had accompanied the supervisor to the post on the night of the incident revealed that the deceased frequently argued with Ramesh, and they never seemed to get along. Apparently, all those arguments took place when they were both under the influence of alcohol.

The Sepoy also mentioned that Basappa, the other guard, was generally very reserved, avoiding getting into any kind of arguments and remaining neutral in the affairs of others. Further questioning of other witnesses corroborated those observations.

It also came to our attention that Sepoy Ramesh had complained of severe knee pain a few days prior to the incident and had even visited the hospital for treatment.

We questioned Ramesh with those additional details, and he revealed that a few days before the incident, he had overslept during his duty shift. Sepoy Kumar became furious and struck him on the knee with the butt of his rifle in an attempt to wake him up. Ramesh claimed it was a minor injury, something he dismissed then and there itself without carrying forward.

Digging deeper, we discovered that some of the other guards had taunted him about that incident later, mocking him with comments like, 'Sher ban kar, tum ek chuhe se maar khaliya?' (Being a lion, you got beaten by a mouse?)

When we pieced the details together and pressed him further, he finally confessed. The humiliation and insult he had endured in front of his peers had become unbearable, and he had been waiting for an opportunity to give it back.

On that fateful night, fuelled by alcohol, he shot Kumar with the victim's own rifle. The sound of the gunshot blended with the crackle of Diwali fireworks, masking the crime.

Afterward, he woke Basappa, who had been sleeping in a nearby tent, and convinced him that their colleague had committed suicide, asking him to inform the supervisor back at the billet.

We completed the formalities, placed the blame on Ramesh and a few others in the chain for their respective lapses, and submitted our inquiry report.

A week later, another officer was assigned by the commander to review the evidence—a necessary step before moving forward with the court martial procedure.

Perhaps fearing severe punishment for the crime he had committed, the accused vehemently denied all allegations before the officer. With a tone of desperation, he claimed, "The officer who conducted the CoI didn't know Hindi, and I didn't know English. Whatever I said, they couldn't understand, and whatever they said, I couldn't grasp either. In all the confusion, they twisted everything and pinned the blame on me!"

*****

I remember another investigation that I found quite amusing but couldn't conclude.

The defence forces take great care of their personnel and their families, with organizations like the Air Force Wives Welfare Association (AFWWA) playing a crucial role. At the unit level, this organization is typically led by the commanding officer's wife. The association regularly interacts with families, providing them with a platform to raise their concerns. If a soldier's spouse has a grievance, they simply need to bring it to AFWWA's attention. The association steps in, examines the case, takes it up with the unit administration, and ensures the matter is addressed and resolved amicably, offering support wherever needed.

While stationed at a unit in Mumbai, a Junior Commissioned Officer's (JCO) wife lodged a complaint with the AFWWA, alleging that, in her absence, another woman was living in his quarter, asserting to be his wife. The administration swiftly categorized the matter as a 'plural marriage case,' and the responsibility of conducting the inquiry fell to me.

The complainant, who was residing in her hometown, had lodged her grievance over the phone. Before proceeding with the inquiry, I decided to verify the facts. My first step was to check the official records maintained by the adjutant. Sure enough, the documents confirmed that the woman who filed the complaint was officially listed as the JCO's wife.

Our inquiry revealed that the JCO had been occupying a quarter despite not being entitled to one, as his family wasn't residing with him. When questioned about it, his responses were evasive, raising further suspicion.

His neighbours confirmed that a woman, claiming to be his wife, frequently stayed with him. However, when we showed them photos of his legal wife from the official records, they hesitated—unable to confirm if she was the same person.

Sensing something amiss, we decided to contact his wife for clarity on the matter and proceed with the inquiry accordingly.

For several days, pressing matters demanded our attention, pushing the inquiry to the back burner. In the meantime, the JCO took a short leave, citing a family emergency, and went to his hometown.

A week later, when we resumed our investigation, we reached out to his legal wife over phone and confirmed that she had never stayed at the station. Armed with that new information, we confronted the JCO.

Under questioning, he admitted that a woman often visited him but insisted she was his father's second wife. To support his claim, he produced a marriage certificate of his father and the said woman, issued by the village Sarpanch.

As additional proof, he produced what he claimed was a wedding photo. In the picture, an elderly man sat at one end of a bench, while a young woman occupied the other—separated by nearly two feet. Both wore garlands, a customary symbol of marriage, yet everything else about the image told a different story. Their faces were turned away from each other, their expressions devoid of any connection, making them look more like strangers sharing a bench than a newlywed couple.

We reached out to a few of his neighbours at the station, hoping they could identify the woman in the photo. Their response was swift and certain—they immediately recognized her as the same woman who had been frequently seen visiting the JCO at his quarters.

It didn't take long to unravel the truth—he had illicitly obtained the marriage certificate from the Sarpanch and staged the photograph as a smokescreen to conceal his actions. However, to take the investigation further, we needed the involvement of his father, the woman, and the Sarpanch. However, summoning them for questioning was beyond our jurisdiction.

With no viable options left, we concluded the inquiry and recommended transferring the case to the civil police for further investigation. Additionally, we proposed revoking his quarter allotment and ensuring that a portion of his salary was directed to his legal wife as a maintenance grant.

When the report reached Headquarters, they acted swiftly and issued an immediate posting for the JCO to a remote non-family station in the Northeast.

They likely thought—"Since his legal wife wasn't planning to join him, let's make sure the other woman doesn't get the chance either."

DUTIES WITH A TWIST

Every military officer is likely to have performed the Liaison Officer duty at some point, mostly while in the junior ranks. That role typically involves being attached to a visiting VIP or a team, tasked with coordinating their schedule and ensuring everything runs smoothly during their visit to a station.

During my posting in Gwalior, the Commander-in-Chief from the Command Headquarters under which our station operated came for an official visit.

As the highest-ranking officer in the Command, he was a figure of immense importance. Every aspect of the station—operations, administration, and even the career progression of officers—rested heavily on his evaluation. His visit naturally placed the Unit Commanders on high alert, each doing everything in their power to ensure no detail was overlooked.

I was assigned as the Liaison Officer for that particular visit. Our station Commander was visibly on edge, anxiously hoping that the entire visit would proceed without even a minor hiccup. He knew the visit was highly crucial for his path ahead in the forces.

During my detailed briefing, he mentioned a few specific habits of the visiting VIP—one that stood out to me was his unwavering routine of taking an evening walk.

I was instructed to politely ask if he wished me to accompany him, with the unspoken understanding that if he agreed, my presence was non-negotiable. Being quite active in sports and games back then, I naively assumed it would be a cakewalk.

His visits to various offices during the day went without a hitch and he was quite pleased with everything. As we were returning to the guest house, he mentioned his plans for the evening walk, adding, "If you don't have any other commitments, please join me."

I arrived at the guest house in PT kit, ten minutes before the scheduled time. He stepped out, right on time, dressed in PT kit, and we began our walk along the station's perimeter road.

Soon, I realized that the walk was much tougher than I had anticipated. He was quite tall, walking briskly on his long legs, and I had to take almost two steps to match his stride. Even at that fast pace, he continued asking about the buildings we passed, while I struggled to catch my breath and respond.

By the time we returned to the guest house, we had covered eight kilometres around the camp, all within about an hour. Exhausted and still panting from the exertion, I requested permission to leave.

As he acknowledged my request, the commander, who was soon to celebrate his sixtieth birthday, offered a piece of advice with a grin: "Young man! Did I trouble you too much? I am sorry. Yet, I advice you to work on your fitness!"

Hearing his advice, all the pride and ego I had as a sportsman instantly evaporated.

*****

Being a Liaison Officer isn't just about following the instructions—it often requires reading your guest's mind and acting accordingly. I once found myself in a rather peculiar situation.

During my tenure in Trivandrum, our station was assigned the responsibility of hosting a VIP and his wife, who had arrived in the state capital on an official visit.

Kerala is renowned for its Ayurvedic treatments and massage therapies, celebrated for their revitalizing and rejuvenating effects. Word of those therapies had likely travelled far, even reaching the corridors of power in Delhi. Perhaps that was why the visiting VIP was keen to experience it first-hand during his stay in Trivandrum. Accordingly, he had arranged an appointment at a prestigious Ayurvedic spa in Kovalam, eager to indulge in Kerala's famed wellness traditions.

I was assigned as the Liaison Officer, to coordinate the security arrangements and to ensure smooth conduct of the VIP at the spa.

I arrived at the resort an hour early to familiarize myself with the place and iron out any potential issues. While speaking with the spa staff, they posed an unexpected query: they offered both male and female therapists, and wanted to know the preference of the VIP and his wife in advance.

Suddenly, I found myself in a dilemma, caught between the proverbial devil and the deep sea. Time was ticking, and I had to make a decision. I decided to address the easier part first.

"For madam, please assign a female therapist," I told them confidently. After a brief pause, I added, "For the VIP, I'll confirm shortly."

Unsure of how to proceed, I called my boss at the headquarters. His response wasn't particularly reassuring: "It's better to ask him directly, but do it discreetly."

The suggestion made sense, but I wasn't sure how the VIP would react—especially if I brought it up in front of his wife. I didn't want to make the wrong choice either.

When the VIP and his wife finally arrived, the manager of the resort greeted them with a traditional Kerala garland at the entrance. From there, I took over and led them to the spa, where they were served a pre-therapy herbal drink.

I was on high alert, looking for the right moment to unnoticeably ask the VIP about his preference. However, his wife remained by his side, leaving no opportunity for a private conversation. Meanwhile, the spa staff hovered nearby, anxious for a decision.

As time ticked away, I decided to take a chance. Quietly, I explained the situation to the VIP, making sure to keep my tone professional and my words neutral. His wife, sitting right next to him, couldn't help but smile at the awkwardness of it all.

The VIP looked at me, seemingly amused by my predicament, and replied with a calm, almost amused tone, "It's fine. Either option is ok with me. It doesn't matter."

That was all I needed. His subtle tone and the knowing smile on his wife's face provided the answer I was looking for. With confidence, I informed the spa manager of his choice of therapist and then retreated to the coffee shop in the courtyard.

*****

While posted at the Headquarters in Trivandrum, my active involvement in various games earned me an additional responsibility as the Command Sports Officer.

In that role, I was responsible for developing sports infrastructure across various units under the Headquarters' jurisdiction. Another key aspect of my responsibilities was identifying and training talented athletes to represent our Command in various disciplines at Air Force-level competitions. A team of coaches, all former service level players, was available to organize coaching camps and prepare various teams.

We frequently collaborated with the State Sports Directorate, utilizing their facilities to train our athletes and host inter-command level competitions. Such a partnership was built on mutual support and a cordial relationship, with both sides offering help to each other whenever needed.

On one occasion, I was invited as a guest for the inaugural ceremony of the State Junior Handball Championship held at Trivandrum. Although attending such events wasn't exactly my preference, I decided to go, mindful of maintaining the healthy rapport we shared with the State Sports Council.

Accompanied by our handball coach—a former services player from Haryana—I arrived at the venue well ahead of the scheduled start. After exchanging pleasantries with the sports council members, we took our seats in a pavilion by the field. The scene before us was vibrant—district teams stood in neat rows, their colourful jerseys adding to the excitement as they eagerly awaited the event's kick off.

Everyone patiently waited for the arrival of the chief guest—a state minister, for formally inaugurating the championship. An announcement was made soon intimating that there was a few minutes of delay for the arrival of the chief guest.

We waited patiently for nearly half an hour more. Another announcement followed soon, intimating about a further ten minutes of delay. Meanwhile, someone from the organisers called for my handball coach back stage.

Another five minutes went by. Then they intimated that the minister wouldn't be able to make it for the function, and without causing inconvenience to those gathered, they had decided to proceed with the function. I felt relieved and grateful that the wait would soon be over.

The announcer began calling the guests—politicians and a few state coaches—one by one to take the seats on the stage. To my utter surprise, my name echoed through the loudspeakers. Caught off guard, I hesitated briefly before reluctantly making my way to the stage.

As I approached, a cute little girl stepped forward, holding a flower brooch in her hand. With a courteous smile, she handed it to me as a gracious gesture of welcome. I thanked her and took a seat among the other distinguished guests, still a bit surprised to find myself in the spotlight.

Our coach came up behind me and murmured, "Sir, they're insisting that you inaugurate the event."

I was stunned and gave him a startled look. He sheepishly continued, "Sir, it's my fault. Thinking I'd earn you some accolades, I told them earlier that you were a former member of the Air Force handball team. I never imagined it would lead to this. With the minister absent, they figured you were the best choice to do the honours."

I knew there was no way out, so I reluctantly nodded in agreement. Just as I was beginning to process the shock, an even bigger one followed—an announcement inviting me to deliver the inaugural address before officially kicking off the event.

I felt my heart skip a beat as I walked mechanically toward the podium, my mind scrambling for words. Public speaking—especially extempore—had never been my forte. Had I known in advance, I would have surely prepared something. But at that moment, there was no room for excuses.

Hiding my apprehension behind a composed exterior, I stood before the microphone. Drawing inspiration from the great orators I had observed, I began, "My dear children and the esteemed guests gathered here..." Then, switching to the comfort of my mother tongue, Malayalam, I spoke for a few minutes. The applause that followed when I finished was probably from the relief that the speech was finally over.

Next, I moved to the field, shook hands with the team captains, and ceremonially picked up the ball. Aiming for one of the goalposts, I threw it with all the flair I could muster. The ball soared through the humid air, curved slightly, and landed squarely in the net. The crowd erupted in cheers, and with that, the championship was officially inaugurated.

I quickly returned to the stage, watched the match for ten minutes and then excused myself with a fabricated story about an urgent office work, and made my way to the car.

The coach caught up with me and said in an excited tone, "Sir that was a fabulous speech— truly motivating!"

I glanced at him, my irritation at being dragged into that situation still evident. While walking, I tried to recall what I had said in my speech but couldn't.

I couldn't help but wonder how that guy from Haryana, who obviously didn't know a word of Malayalam, could confidently declare it was fantastic!

*****

Additional responsibilities in the military were not always pleasant; some can be profoundly emotional.

In the armed forces, when a member tragically passes away, the parent unit ensures full support is extended to the grieving family—for the funeral and beyond. If the family decides to relocate to any other place, the nearest Air Force unit is tasked with providing all necessary assistance to complete the documentation and other formalities. It is also customary for the Air Force Chief to convey condolences, often through a written message, which the local unit is responsible for delivering personally to the bereaved family.

While posted in Bangalore, I was entrusted with one such task. The previous week, an officer had tragically lost his life in an accident while serving at a unit in Punjab. After the funeral, his wife and their two-year-old son had moved to Bangalore to stay with her in-laws.

A letter of condolence addressed to the widow of the officer soon arrived at my unit, and I was assigned to deliver it.

Their home, situated in a quiet, sparsely populated area, was easy to find. Dressed in uniform, my introduction was far easier and I explained the purpose of my visit. The family—a grieving wife, her toddler son, the officer's aged parents, and his sister—was still visibly grappling with the loss.

I expressed my heartfelt condolences and handed over the letter of condolence. Before leaving, I provided the unit's contact information and assured her that we were available for any assistance they might need.

Two days later, the officer's father and sister came to my office. He looked completely shaken, still struggling to cope with the loss. They had brought all the necessary documents for processing the insurance claim, gratuity, and family pension—duly filled out and signed. In such cases, the unit commander of the nearest Air Force unit had to review the documents, verify the signatures, and then forward it to Headquarters for approval.

Noticing the officer's wife wasn't with them, I casually inquired about her. They replied that she had gone to stay with her parents for a few days.

After quickly glancing through the documents, I assured them that the verification would be completed within a day or two and that I would inform them if any additional documents or signatures were needed.

Upon scrutinizing the papers, we found that a few signatures were missing on some documents. Not wanting to trouble them again, I sent a clerk to their residence the next day to collect the required signatures.

However, he returned without success, as the parents were not at home. He also mentioned that the officer's wife was present but seemed unaware of the paperwork being processed. That raised concerns, so I decided to call the officer's unit in Punjab for clarification.

The response I received did confirm my fears. The officer had not updated his will after marriage, and the nominees listed in the documents were still his parents. They also confirmed that the necessary documents had been handed over to the officer's parents, while they were there for the funeral.

It became evident to me that the parents were proceeding with the claims independently, without involving the officer's wife. That discovery was deeply unsettling. If the situation remained as it was, the officer's widow might have had to pursue never ending legal battles to claim her rightful share. Perhaps the aged parents needed the financial support too, or they feared that their daughter-in-law might remarry, diverting the funds to another family.

Yet, if she chose not to remarry, what then? Even if she remarried later, how was she going to sail through the rough patch at the moment?

Whatever their reasoning, it was clear to me that the widow and her young child needed the support the most at that critical juncture. I reached out to a friend handling pay and pensions at Delhi Headquarters and discussed the case. He informed me that similar situations in the past had led to the implementation of a system ensuring that the wife would automatically be included as a beneficiary.

While it might not have completely resolved the situation, I hoped it would bring some measure of solace to the young widow.

*****

Every year, the IAF stations all over celebrates Air Force Day in a grand way. It is customary to invite retired officers living in and around the station to join the dinner party at the Officers' Mess. For the veterans, it's a cherished occasion—a chance to step back into their familiar world, reconnect with old comrades, and relive the memories in uniform.

In the forces, everything is done in an orderly manner—hosts are assigned in advance, each responsible for a couple of guests. They ensure that the guests are well taken care of throughout the evening, from welcoming them upon arrival to engaging in lively conversations, as well as ensuring drinks and snacks are served without interruption. It is a routine we follow year after year, but my first experience as a host remains unforgettable.

I was assigned to look after an eighty-year-old veteran and his wife. After welcoming them at the entrance of the mess lawn, where the party was being held, I engaged them in a small talk, got them their desired drinks, and made sure they were comfortable.

As the evening progressed, they mingled with others while I moved around yet always kept a watchful eye on them. My veteran guest had a fondness for Old Monk rum with ice and soda. Each time I noticed the drink in his glass dipped below the halfway mark, I discreetly sent a waiter with a refill. The moment he saw the next drink lined up on the tray in front of him, he'd quickly gulp down whatever remained in his glass and grab the next one. I took pride in being the perfect host, ensuring his glass was never empty.

In between those little moments when I observed they were lacking company, I would rush over, playing the attentive listener to his endless stories, until someone else joined the conversation. In about an hour and a half, the old gentleman had downed six or seven drinks—and was still going strong.

At one point, he leaned toward me and asked, "Where's the loo?"

The washrooms were inside the mess building, and considering his age and the number of drinks he'd had, I figured it would be difficult for him to get there unassisted. I offered to accompany him, and off we went—he, dragging himself forward on shaky legs, and I, closely following, ready to spring into action should he stumble.

Once we reached the washroom, he stepped inside and positioned himself in front of a urinal while I waited outside. A minute passed. Then two. Then five. Ten.

I started getting worried. I stepped in to check and found him still standing there, seemingly frozen in place, his frail frame leaning slightly against the partition. Assuming he was just taking his time to relieve himself after all the drinks he had consumed, I waited a little longer. But after another couple of minutes with no change, my concern began to grow. I walked up to him and called out softly. No response.

I gently tapped his shoulder. That did the trick. He stirred slightly, blinking as if waking from a deep slumber. Then, without a word, he straightened up and made his way back to the lawn, with me trailing behind.

That little nap must have revitalized him—he looked fresh, back to his usual self, chatting with his colleagues and clearly ready for a few more drinks. However, I wasn't willing to take any more chances. Fearing another 'loo crisis,' I quietly ensured that no waiter approached him with another drink for the rest of the evening!

PART AND PARCELL

There were plenty of other duties which needed to be performed regularly by every defence officer, each with its own quirks and challenges! Here's a glimpse of a few of them.

Until the late nineties, troop salaries were primarily disbursed in cash, mostly in hundred and ten rupee denominations. In a large station with over two thousand personnel, there were typically seven or eight designated pay points, each managed by an officer on rotation.

On payday—typically the last working day of the month—the assigned officer would receive a bag containing the total salary for his pay point. He was responsible for distributing the cash, recording each transaction in individual pay books, and reconciling the total payment before returning any unclaimed balance to the accounts section.

Handling five to ten lakh rupees in small denominations was no easy task, especially for officers unaccustomed to counting large sums manually. Errors were always a looming threat. If there was a shortfall after tallying, the officer had to cover it from his own pocket—painful but harmless. However, a surplus was far worse. It indicated that someone had been underpaid, a serious lapse that could trigger an inquiry.

And if you thought you could quietly pocket the excess and walk away, think again! The accounts department often identified miscalculations on their end during the final reconciliation, which could suddenly turn a surplus into a deficiency—leaving you answerable for that too!

Another duty that came with its fair share of drama was that of the Range Duty Officer—the one responsible for overseeing weapon firing exercises at the range. Tasked with ensuring safety, he worked alongside Ground Training Instructors (GTIs) and Weapon Fitter tradesmen—the specialists in handling and maintaining firearms.

Before firing practice commenced, a thorough briefing was mandatory. Thereafter, the guards would be deployed at every corner of the range, red flags in hand, to prevent anyone from wandering into the danger zone.

Every round of ammunition was meticulously accounted for. Each participant had to collect rounds from the local armoury and return an equal number of empty shells after firing. Losing even a single shell was a nightmare—it meant uncertainty about whether the round had been fired or was still out there, potentially posing a deadly risk.

And that meant only one thing—no one was leaving the range until the empty shell was found! The entire range would be combed, grain by grain, until the missing shell was recovered—sometimes taking many extra hours.

The range duty often led to tense encounters with the local villagers too. Residents living near the range eagerly awaited the end of firing sessions. The moment the team left, they would rush in, digging through the soil around the range to collect valuable lead fragments from spent bullets.

During one of my range duties, everything went smoothly— or so I thought—until we returned to the base. Later that afternoon, a middle-aged man arrived at the station with his young son, who had an injury on his right knee. He claimed the boy had been hit by a stray bullet while playing near the range and demanded money for hospital treatment.

The IAF police examined the wound and immediately sensed something was off. It didn't resemble a bullet injury but rather looked like one from a fall. They decided to escalate the matter to the civil police. At that moment, the boy, visibly shaken, blurted out the truth—he had injured himself while running to collect lead pieces with his friends. Realizing their bluff had been exposed, the father grabbed the boy and disappeared quickly from the guardroom.

Another crucial duty often performed by everyone was that of the Station Duty Officer—the one responsible for the safety and security of the camp after working hours. It was his job to monitor and report any unexpected incidents that arose during his duty hours, while also ensuring that the guards stationed at various security posts remained alert at all times.

During the late-night hours, he was required to conduct surprise guard checks at various posts scattered across the vast station boundary, including the remote corners! A strict security protocol was in place, wherein a unique password and counter-password were generated daily by the security department and discreetly distributed to the authorized personnel. Those served as identification keys for anyone approaching a guard post—the visitor had to provide the correct password when challenged by the guard, who would then verify it with the designated counter-password.

Most passwords and counter-passwords were Hindi words, which were tricky for those less fluent in the language. Early on, many of us found ourselves in nerve-wracking situations—standing frozen under the barrel of a gun during a guard check, fumbling to recall the password, and ultimately being subjected to an alternate verification drill.

"Dono haath upar karke, do kadam aage badho!" the guard would shout keeping you always at the gun sight.

Once you complied, he would command again, "ID card bahar nikaal kar neeche rakho!"

"Peeche mud, aur das kadam aage chalo!" The guard would keep the visitor at a safe distance, ensuring he could check the identity card without risking any potential threat.

Once satisfied, he would salute, and say loudly 'Jai Hind Sir' before swiftly extending the guard register for a signature.

Some of us had the habit of doing that intentionally—deliberately withholding the password—to ensure that the guards remained sharp and followed every procedures meticulously, rather than simply assuming that the visitor was the duty officer and rushing through the check!

HAND SHAKE

Every patriotic Indian eagerly looks forward to the 26th of January—the day India proudly became a republic. That significant occasion is marked by the grand Republic Day parade in Delhi, a spectacle that never fails to ignite pride among citizens.

The sight of soldiers in their impeccable military uniforms, adorned with colourful badges and gleaming medals, marching in perfect synchrony to the beat of the drums, is nothing short of mesmerizing. Their headgear, worn with a palpable sense of pride, adds to the grandeur of the event.

Parades are an integral part of military tradition and discipline, and they constitute one of the first lessons every soldier learns during training. Beyond their ceremonial allure, they represent much more—they are a unifying force. The uniform and the disciplined movements of the parade create a bond that transcends regional, cultural, and linguistic differences, uniting individuals from vastly diverse backgrounds under a common purpose and identity.

The military is renowned for its parades, each serving a unique purpose and carrying its own significance. The most familiar, of course, is the grand ceremonial parade often associated with national events.

Another remarkable parade is *'Beating the Retreat'*, a solemn and elegant ceremony marking the conclusion of Republic Day celebrations. Then there's the *'Guard of Honour'*, a meticulously coordinated display presented to dignitaries such as the President, Ministers, and military Commanders.

Equally poignant is the *'Funeral Parade'*, conducted with the utmost respect and precision to honour soldiers who have made the ultimate sacrifice in service to the nation. Each parade reflects the discipline, pride, and deep traditions of military life.

During my posting in Mumbai, I had the privilege of representing the Indian Air Force in numerous parades. Perhaps my lean and athletic build without even a hint of paunch back during those days, coupled with my active involvement in sports, made me an easy pick. Or perhaps it was simply the convenience of routine—whenever the question arose, '*Who did it last time?*' the administration often took the easy route and assigned me again!

Though the commands and drills are uniform across all three military services, each branch dons its distinctive uniform: Olive Green for the Army, White for the Navy, and Blue for the Air Force.

The Army, with its diverse regiments, has minor variations in between them—mainly in headgear and the belts. In contrast, both the Navy and the Air Force have a standardized uniform for all personnel, as there is no regimentation within them.

All the guards in the parade carry a rifle in their right hand. Commanders such as the Parade Commander, Contingent Commander, and Flight Commander are from officer cadre. In the Army and Navy, officers on ceremonial parades carry a sword and execute the entire drill with it.

However, in the Air Force, officers carry a revolver securely tucked inside a holder attached to their belt. The revolver is never drawn during the parade; instead, the entire drill is performed with their bare hands.

During my posting in Mumbai, the newly sworn-in President of India paid a visit to the city. In his honour, a tri-service Guard of Honour was organized at the Mumbai Airport. As Mumbai was primarily a Navy led station, the Guard Commander for the event was an officer from the Indian Navy. The three services—Army, Navy, and Air Force— provided a contingent, each commanded by an officer from their respective branches. I had the privilege of serving as the Air Force Contingent Commander for that prestigious ceremony.

In a tri-service Guard of Honour, the contingents form up in the order of their formation seniority: the Indian Army, being the oldest, takes the lead, followed by the Navy, and finally, the youngest service, the Indian Air Force. Accordingly, we assembled on the tarmac a few minutes before the VIP's arrival, standing in perfect formation.

Towards the end of the Guard of Honour, the VIP customarily inspects the Guards, walking past the contingents in a measured, ceremonial march. Following protocol, the President completed his inspection of the three contingents. At that point, he was supposed to return to the dais, accompanied by the Contingent Commander.

But instead, he turned back and walked directly toward me. Stopping in front of me, he extended his hand for a handshake. That was completely unanticipated—not being part of the prescribed drill.

For a moment, I was taken aback. But what could I do? There was the Supreme Commander of the Armed Forces offering a handshake. Refusing was unthinkable. I immediately extended my hand and shook hand with him. While doing so, he glanced over the three contingents, expressing his pleasure and gratitude for the immaculate display.

Perhaps he wanted to convey his appreciation to the entire contingent with a formal handshake and was looking for an opportunity. In the parade, everyone except me held arms — rifles or swords. Spotting me standing with empty hands, he probably seized the opportunity.

Whatever the reason, that moment became a cherished memory. On a ceremonial parade, I had the rare privilege of shaking hands with our Supreme Commander—a privilege I owe, perhaps, to the Air Force's reliance on modern sophistication and firepower. While others bore traditional swords and rifles, we carried the sleek and powerful revolver, leaving my hand conveniently free for an impromptu gesture of recognition.

YES BOSS

The role of a boss in the defence forces is undeniably significant. Beyond assigning tasks, they wield authority over disciplinary matters, approving leave, and initiating annual confidential reports (ACRs). Those reports, which directly influence career progression, make it imperative for subordinates to stay in their boss's good books—an unspoken rule for anyone seeking a smoother journey in the forces.

ACRs for officers were typically prepared in June and September—June for junior ranks and September for seniors. Those months often saw a spike in social events, as officers scrambled to host parties, hoping to leave a positive impression on their bosses.

After all, throwing a party needed a reason, right? Without one, the true intention would be far too obvious. To sidestep that awkwardness, many officers would creatively 'relocate' their birthdays or anniversaries to align with those months.

In the defence forces, juniors rarely have the luxury of saying '*No.*' Most were primed to respond with an enthusiastic "*Yes, Sir!*" to every word of wisdom—or whim—emanating from their boss. Two unwritten rules seem to govern the dynamic between a boss and their subordinates in military:

Rule 1: 'The boss is always right'.

Rule 2: 'If ever in doubt, refer to Rule 1'.

In fact, many chose to follow those unwritten rules half heartedly, valuing their peace of mind over the perils of resistance.

When the boss endorsed an idea, most chose the safer route of an enthusiastic 'Yes,' their faces lighting up with an expression akin to the famous TV commercial's 'What an idea, Sirji!' However, there were a few brave souls who dared to speak their minds. They critically analysed the boss's proposition, pointed out potential flaws, and suggested alternatives they genuinely believed were better. Unfortunately, the boss's ego often acted as a barrier, making such feedback unwelcome.

More often than not, the boss pressed ahead with his original plan. The agreeable '*Yes Men*' would smartly wriggle out of taking charge of the execution, leaving the lone dissenter—the one courageous enough to voice concerns—shouldering the responsibility of making the idea work.

Ironically, despite their efforts, those dissenters were often disliked by the boss, while the '*Yes Men*' stayed in his good books—not for any meaningful contributions, but simply for their unwavering public agreement with him.

Some bosses wouldn't think twice about using threats to get what they want. I recall one such incident in a unit, where a discussion was underway on a seemingly trivial matter—presenting a gift for an officer leaving the service prematurely. The idea came from the commander, and as expected, the surrounding 'Yes Men' quickly rallied in support. That wasn't a tradition in the service, and a few of us were sceptical. Yet, with the majority nodding along, we thought it wiser to go with the flow.

Around the same time, another short-service officer, a rank junior to the first, was also leaving the service after completing his short service tenure. Someone suggested that we extend the same courtesy to him as well. But then the commander was clearly against it, dismissing the idea as unnecessary since the officer was relatively junior. As expected, his loyalists echoed his opinion. The real reason, however, was apparent—the first officer was very close to the commander, and hence the commander wanted to present a memorable parting gift to him.

Someone decided to speak up against the idea and a few of us who felt it was justified cautiously voiced our support. The commander's deputy, my boss, visibly irate, dragged us out of the room and lashed out: "Don't you know he's senior by a rank to the short-service guy? Someone with more integrity to the service!" he yelled, obviously referring to the two officers. We couldn't help but wonder about his logic regarding integrity—was it simply years of seniority, or something more dubious? The idea was eventually shelved, and those who had rebelled were labelled the villains.

Fate, however, had its way of balancing the scales. Years later, the same officer who had lectured us about integrity found himself convicted for a far graver crime, eventually ended up serving a term of rigorous imprisonment in *Tihar Jail*.

Some bosses have a knack for being contrarians, always suggesting the opposite of what you say—perhaps as a way to assert their authority.

I once worked under a boss like that. If you asked for leave, he'd respond with something like, "There are pressing matters right now. Why don't you postpone it for a few days?"

Eventually, we figured out a way to handle him. Instead of directly asking for leave, we'd say, "Sir, I was planning to take leave next week, but with some upcoming commitments, I'll probably postpone it."

Predictably, he'd counter, "No, no, don't worry about that. You can take your leave next week. I'll manage if anything comes up."

And we'd get exactly what we wanted—by letting his contrarian streak work in our favour!

Some individuals go a step further and prioritize impressing the boss, often at the expense of their colleagues. During parties, I would often volunteer for managing the audio-visual setup—not out of enthusiasm but to avoid two dreaded roles: being the master of ceremonies and participating in the customary dances.

One weekend, just as I was about to head out for a movie with my wife and kids, my phone rang. It was a colleague, who also happened to be the Mess Secretary. "Hello, Mats. There's an issue with the presentation, and the team here can't fix it. The Air Marshal is asking for you. Please come quickly," he urged.

I hesitated, knowing that if I went to the mess, I would miss the movie and likely be stuck there until late into the night. "Sorry, Nat. We're heading out for a movie, and I can't cancel it now," I replied, puzzled as to why they hadn't informed me earlier if my involvement was critical—it didn't seem like a real emergency.

"No, the Air Marshal wants you here now. Please come," he insisted.

Remembering that some colleagues often exaggerated by dropping the boss's name, I said, "Tell him I'm in the city, and it'll take some time for me to get back."

Just as we were locking the door to leave, two colleagues rushed over, visibly worried. They explained the situation: during a practice session, the IT officer had encountered technical issues, and the Air Marshal, who was present, had lost his temper. To save face, they had shifted the blame to me, saying, "Sir, Mats was supposed to handle this, but he hasn't shown up." To make matters worse, the Mess Secretary had called me on speakerphone while sitting right in front of the Air Marshal, who was listening to the entire conversation. My unaware response had only escalated the situation.

Realizing the matter had spiralled out of control, I reluctantly headed to the mess. Upon arrival, I immediately apologized to the Air Marshal and explained the miscommunication.

To my relief, the Air Marshal was gracious. "Back in our day, if an Air Marshal called, we'd drop everything and run," he said with a wry smile. "But it's fine. I know you weren't informed—someone's been playing dirty. I'll handle that. If you have urgent plans, feel free to go."

His fairness left a lasting impression on me. Despite having a personal commitment, I decided to stay behind and offer my support.

MICROSCOPIC EYES

Soldiers are trained to stay ever-vigilant, a habit so deeply ingrained that they remain alert, no matter whether they are on duty or enjoying a break in the comfort of their home.

They have an uncanny ability to observe the surroundings and can detect anything unusual in the blink of an eye. It's almost as if they possess microscopic vision, seeing details far beyond what most others notice.

At every station, there was a clear distinction between the living area and the technical area, the latter being the hub of all operations. Entry into the technical area was strictly controlled, with guests requiring approval from security department.

A station commander was driving into the technical area in his gypsy, the staff flag fluttering at the front, with an elderly man sitting beside him. As the highest authority at the station, everyone recognized him, and usually, the guards would salute and allow him through without a word.

However, the security in charge, stationed at the office, noticed the vehicle approaching from a distance. Quickly, he rushed out and halted the vehicle as it entered the technical area. With a crisp salute, he informed the commander, "Sir, there's an urgent call for you on the exchange extension," pointing to the phone in his office.

Surprised who might be calling, the commander followed him into the office to take the call.

Once inside, the officer, with a hint of apology, explained, "My apologies, Sir. I had to come up with a story to get you here. I noticed an unfamiliar person in the Gypsy with you and wanted to rule out the remote possibility that he might have been holding you hostage to gain entry."

The commander, now understanding, explained it was his father. He praised the young soldier for his sharp observation and quick thinking, recognizing how easily an infiltrator could have used such a tactic to breach security.

Interestingly, those sharp observations often led to amusing outcomes as well, adding a touch of humour to their otherwise serious demeanour.

In Bangalore, a critical server room for the communication network was situated right outside my office. Access to the room was restricted to authorized personnel through a biometric-controlled glass door. A surveillance camera kept a constant watch, recording activity in the area 24/7.

Since the room was located deep within the station, already a highly secure zone, the camera footage wasn't monitored in real time. Instead, like many others, the recordings were stored for review only if needed.

One morning, as I was leaving my office, I noticed a man in civilian attire standing near the server room door. Given the number of civilians working in nearby offices, I assumed he was one of them. When he spotted me, he promptly greeted me with a 'Jai Hind,' reinforcing my assumption. I returned his greeting and continued on my way, not giving the encounter much thought.

Later, upon returning, curiosity got the better of me. I decided to review the surveillance footage to see who he was. The recording showed him lingering near the server room for nearly an hour, occasionally peering through the glass door. His demeanour suggested unease, even panic. I shared the footage with a few colleagues, but no one recognized him.

Sensing that something was amiss, I immediately reported the incident to the security department. They reviewed the recording but were also unable to identify the individual. Concerned, they escalated the matter to the commander.

Within minutes, an alert was issued, and the campus was placed on high alert. Assuming the man could be an intruder possibly still within the premises, security personnel launched a thorough search.

After nearly an hour, they found the 'suspect' in a cafeteria. He turned out to be a civilian cook posted at a nearby unit, visiting the headquarters for a loan approval.

He had arrived by an auto-rickshaw but found himself unable to pay the fare, as his wallet was empty. Hoping to borrow money from a friend, he wandered the campus but couldn't locate him. In order to evade the auto driver, he chose the area near the server room as a makeshift hideout—right where I had spotted him.

Once the misunderstanding was resolved, the alert was lifted. While the incident turned out to be harmless, it wasn't entirely in vain. It served as an excellent drill, sharpening everyone's security awareness and response skills.

On another occasion, while posted in Mumbai, an unusual incident added an interesting twist to a December evening.

I was out for a stroll with my two sons—the younger one nestled in my arms and the elder one cheerfully pedalling his little cycle beside me.

As we passed the parade ground, my younger son's eyes lit up at the sight of a pigeon hopping around in the corner. Eager to give him a closer look, I moved nearer. The pigeon seemed distressed, flapping its wings weakly in failed attempts to fly. Something appeared to be tangled around its tiny legs.

On closer inspection, I discovered a tiny roll of paper tied to its leg. It instantly reminded me of the messenger pigeons I had read about—those remarkable birds that carried messages back and forth long before modern communication systems came into existence. Seeing one in real life was thrilling, and I eagerly shared the story with my curious kids.

A sudden question flashed through my mind: "Who could possibly be using messenger pigeons in this modern era?"

I remembered a recent security briefing, discussing the evolving tactics of certain terrorist groups. "Could this be part of such a scheme?" The thought intrigued me.

Immediately, I alerted the station's security officer. Within minutes, the security team arrived, closely followed by the station commander. They found the hapless pigeon still struggling, its efforts growing more frantic as the crowd started gathering around. All eyes fell on the note tied to its leg, and the suspicion that I had seemed to be reflecting in everyone's mind.

The commander ordered that the bird be caught at all costs. The security staff approached cautiously, but the pigeon hopped farther each time, evading capture. Concerned it might take flight and disappear, they abandoned chasing it. A marksman soon arrived, armed as a precaution to shoot the bird if it tried to fly away.

Meanwhile, someone brought a few plastic nets, which they spread strategically around the parade ground, scattering handfuls of grains to lure the pigeon.

The team waited patiently, keeping a safe distance to avoid startling the bird. After about thirty tense minutes, the pigeon cautiously approached the net, pecking at the grains. Moments later, its legs got entangled on the net, and the security staff swiftly captured it. They removed the note and handed it over to the commander.

As the commander unfolded the note, it unveiled a reality entirely different from our grave assumptions. It wasn't a sinister message between miscreants but a love letter—a heartfelt expression from the teenage son of an officer to the daughter of another.

The boy, smitten by his classmate, had struggled to convey his feelings. In his desperation, he devised a whimsical plan: capturing a pigeon from his balcony, he penned his emotions onto a piece of paper, tied it to the bird's leg, and set it free.

He knew the message would never reach its intended recipient but found solace in the act itself. Little did he know, his romantic gesture would create a security spectacle that just got unfolded.

BENEATH THE CANVAS ROOF

It's no exaggeration to say, '*A soldier is always on the move.*' It is true not only for transfers or new postings but even while stationed at a unit. Operational demands often arise unexpectedly, requiring soldiers to mobilize at short notice—sometimes within just hours.

Anticipating such eventualities, every soldier makes it a habit to keep an overnight bag packed and ready. It's a familiar scene in military households for children to wake up and ask, "*Where is Papa?*" Their mother, with a resigned smile or a knowing sigh, would reply, "*He's on TD.*" The kids understood what that meant: TD, or Temporary Duty –it could be days, or in some cases, even weeks before their father returned home.

Until he returned, the responsibility of managing the household rested entirely on the capable shoulders of the women. They ensured everything ran seamlessly, sparing their husbands from every domestic concerns. Instead, they became pillars of strength, offering unwavering support and boosting their morale, allowing the soldiers to focus wholeheartedly on their duty to the nation.

Moving to another unit was relatively hassle-free, with the mess typically taking care of the necessary arrangements. However, operational deployments to remote locations—often vast stretches of open land hundreds of kilometres away with no established infrastructure—presented an entirely different set of challenges.

The designated campsite was often an isolated stretch of government land, either along a coastal line or atop a hill, strategically chosen based on the operational requirement.

Everyone knew that once deployed, it could be weeks or even months before they returned to the safety of their parent base. Hence they carried everything to make the camp life as smooth as possible. Alongside the operational necessities such as machinery, arms, and ammunition, they packed everything needed for daily life—tents, furniture, utensils, coolers, fans, generators, and even TV sets—ensuring they could create a functional and sustainable home away from home, no matter how far from comfort they were.

The moment the siren sounded, everything quickly gets loaded onto the trucks, soldiers climb on and the convoy is ready to move. Each one knew their role to perfection, a result of countless drills and meticulous practice that ensured seamless execution.

The gruelling hours or even days of travel from the base did nothing to dampen the soldiers' resolve. Upon arrival, they wasted no time turning the desolate landscape into a thriving, self-sufficient outpost. It became their temporary home, though its duration remained uncertain.

The camp setup was thoughtfully arranged to ensure a comfortable stay. Tents of various sizes catered to different needs, from compact accommodations for individuals to larger ones serving as dining halls or recreation rooms. Each tent was layered for protection—a rugged olive-green tarpaulin outer to shield against rain and heat, and a thick fabric inner layer for insulation. Sturdy sidewalls enclosed the tents, while *durries* (jute carpets) covered the ground to protect against mud and dust.

Each tent was equipped with essential amenities—fans, coolers, or heaters—carefully chosen to suit the prevailing climate and provide some measure of comfort in an otherwise harsh environment. Snake pits were dug around the tents, to prevent reptiles from creeping in.

The camp featured amenities like a reading room, a TV room, and indoor games such as carom and chess. Those simple comforts offered a much-needed respite from the rigorous duty, bringing moments of relaxation and mental rejuvenation.

A volleyball court was an essential feature of every camp, injecting energy and camaraderie into the evenings. The friendly matches not only lifted spirits but also strengthened bonds among the soldiers, making the camp life more vibrant and enjoyable.

Tents were meticulously camouflaged using jute nets and tree branches, allowing them to blend seamlessly into the surrounding terrain. The careful concealment minimized the risk of detection by enemy aircraft during potential air raids.

Armed guards maintained a vigilant round-the-clock watch, providing a steadfast layer of protection for the camp and its occupants.

The cookhouse was another hub of activity, serving freshly prepared meals to the camp. Dry rations were sourced weekly from the nearest unit, while fresh produce like vegetables and milk was procured from local markets. For those who enjoyed an evening drink, a makeshift mini bar operated from the dining hall before dinner hours.

Establishing a liaison with local authorities or the village *Sarpanch* helped in fostering goodwill within the community besides ensuring essential resources like electricity and water to the camp.

Modern toilet luxuries were, of course, non-existent in camp life. Instead, everyone relied on makeshift camp toilets set up a bit far away from the camp site in a secluded corner. Wooden planks with a central opening were placed over deep trenches, forming the basic structure.

There were two types: the Single Trench Latrine (STL), which featured a single unit, and the Multiple Trench Latrine (MTL), consisting of several units arranged in a row, each separated by a simple partition.

For privacy, hessian cloth walls were draped around wooden poles fixed at the four corners, and another piece of hessian cloth hung at the entrance, acting as a makeshift door for easy access.

Water for the necessary clean up used to be carried in empty liquor bottles. However, no water was used to flush the toilet. Instead, the waste would be covered with a mixture of dry sand and lime kept in a corner, using a shovel kept aside for the task.

Privacy was another challenge, as there was no provision to bolt the toilet from the inside. Some patient souls might attempt to tie the door flap to the poles, but that was hardly fool proof. To address that, a practical system was implemented: the occupant would either sing loudly or hang a towel at the entrance as a signal. That simple rule, followed with humour and mutual understanding, became an essential part of camp life.

Once, while deployed at a site along the coastline on the western border, we noticed that many locals had a habit of using the shore for their morning rituals. When they saw us setting up camp nearby, they probably assumed that, from then on, we'd be competing with them for space on the already crowded beach. Fortunately, we had our own camp toilets—the trusty STLs and MTLs.

As a goodwill gesture, we set up a few MTLs for the locals a little farther away. Initially, they were hesitant to use them, but with some persuasion from local leaders, most gradually made the switch. As a result, the stretch of shore remained clean and litter-free. That once-cluttered beach soon became our own little oasis—a perfect spot for beach cricket and the occasional refreshing dip in the Arabian Sea!

Once we had to set up a camp on a hilltop at the edge of the *Borivilli National Park*. Leopards, often venturing into nearby villages in search of prey, particularly dogs, were a common sight in the area.

Soon, they began appearing around our camp too, spreading unease among the soldiers. No one dared to venture out of the campus especially after the sunset. Before turning in for the night, everyone ensured their tent doors were securely tied to the hooks. Some even slept with loaded rifles by their side, as a precaution against the unexpected.

The camp toilets, positioned a little away from the main site, became a no-go zone after dark. Anyone needing to venture there at night never did so alone—it was practically a tactical mission. Two armed escorts would accompany the individual, standing guard outside, their eyes scanning the darkness, fingers resting on the triggers of their rifles, ready to fire at anything that emerged from the surrounding bushes! Probably none ever had the luxury—before or after—of being guarded by armed escorts while answering nature's call!

The presence of leopards was likely encouraged by the street dogs that frequented the camp, drawn by the hope of food scraps. As the dogs lingered, so did the leopards. Night guards began spotting them more frequently. At first, the creatures would bolt when caught in the beam of a flashlight, but soon enough, they grew accustomed to the light and stopped reacting altogether.
On many nights, we spotted one sitting calmly on a nearby rock, observing the camp's activities with a composed curiosity. Sleep became elusive for most of us. In an attempt to deter the leopard, we decided to fire false rounds, hoping the sound would scare it away. Yet, the leopard seemed unimpressed. Once the firing ceased, they would leisurely rise, retreat behind the bushes, and vanish into the darkness.

It almost felt as though the leopard understood the Indian soldier's restraint—knowing that even in that unusual encounter, it wouldn't be harmed. Or perhaps it figured sitting still was a safer bet than fleeing and risking a stray bullet. The leopard continued its nocturnal visits for several days, always maintaining a curious but harmless presence.

Strangely enough, it caused no trouble to anyone in the camp. Perhaps, in its own way, it was adding an extra layer of security to the Indian military camp—a silent guardian from the wild.

BATTLES IN THE SAND

Science students might recall learning about the '*Annealing Process*' in their chemistry classes—a technique where metal is heated to a high temperature and then rapidly cooled to enhance its mechanical properties. A desert posting, in many ways, mirrored that process — not on any metal, but on the human body and spirit.

To witness summer in its most merciless form, one must experience life in a desert. The relentless heat, often soaring past 50 degrees Celsius, makes existence almost unbearable. Adding to the misery, fierce sandstorms sweep across the vast dunes, carrying clouds of fine sand that infiltrate everything.

Those expecting winter to bring relief would be sorely mistaken. Desert winters plunge to the opposite extreme, with night-time temperatures frequently dipping below freezing. Just as the body begins to recover from the biting cold, summer creeps in, kicking off yet another cycle of 'annealing,' further refining resilience and endurance.

The vast deserts of Rajasthan were dotted with numerous military units, and for anyone in the Army or Air Force, a desert posting was an experience they simply couldn't miss. It was an unparalleled test of strength, adaptability, and camaraderie. I was no exception—my posting brought me to a unit situated just a stone's throw away from the India-Pakistan border.

Life in the desert was anything but easy, with the relentless extremes of weather alternating between scorching summers and bone-chilling winters. The only reprieve came during the brief transition period between the two—a fleeting few weeks of mild weather.

It was in that short-lived window that rain, a rare visitor to the arid expanse, would grace the land. For the desert's parched inhabitants, each drop of rain was a treasured blessing. Yet, the desert had its quirks. Beneath the sand lay a thick layer of gypsum, impervious to water. As a result, even a few hours of rain could transform the landscape into sprawling lakes, giving it a weird temporary makeover.

For a South Indian like me, reaching the desert station was no less than a Herculean task. The nearest cities were Jodhpur, about 200 kilometres to the East, and Ahmedabad, roughly 400 kilometres to the South. Back then, connectivity to the main line at Jodhpur depended largely on a meter-gauge train that stopped at every village along its route.

To reach Kochi, I had two options: travel via Delhi or Ahmedabad, both requiring an overnight journey before catching another train southward. When traveling alone, I often took the direct state transport buses to Ahmedabad to save time, though it was far from comfortable.

Those buses were perpetually packed to the brim with passengers in their traditional attire, carrying everything from bicycles and livestock to sacks of *bajra* and bundles of cotton. Despite traveling numerous times and encountering hundreds of faces, I noticed the same blank expression on almost everyone. While they would observe newcomers with quiet curiosity, they rarely smiled, merely shifting slightly to make room on the already crowded seats.

The open top deck of the bus, often more crowded than the interior, always intrigued me. Perhaps the passengers were recreating the experience of a camel ride through the desert, or maybe they were drawn to it by the allure of a cheaper ticket. Whatever the reason, those journeys were not just challenging but also unforgettable, offering a fascinating glimpse into the vibrant and resilient spirit of desert life.

When traveling with family, many preferred driving to Jodhpur and then to catch train for the onward journey. Driving in the desert was an experience as light and effortless as a feather. For most of the journey, the road stretched ahead endlessly, straight as an arrow, cutting smoothly through the sand dunes. Traffic was almost non-existent, and the drive required minimal effort—no steering around bends or frequent gear shifts. Just hold the wheel steady, press the accelerator, and let the car glide.

Occasionally, a distant 'mountain' would emerge on the horizon, inching closer with every passing moment. As it drew near, the illusion would fade, revealing a tractor hauling a small trolley overloaded with an enormous pile of *bajra* straw, spilling over to nearly cover the entire width of the road. Those were the rare moments that required full attention—you'd need to slow down and give way. Failing to do so might result in your car ploughing through the heap, with a generous portion of straw adorning your roof!

At times, you'd encounter a herd of sheep casually blocking the road, leaving you with no choice but to stop. The flock seemed to hold their ground, almost as if protesting your presence. After honking a few times, the shepherd would eventually appear from nowhere, calmly guiding the flock to one side, allowing your car to pass.

However, there was always the looming risk of a vehicle breakdown, which could leave you stranded in the vast desert with no help in sight. In those moments, you could only whisper a prayer, hoping for another vehicle to come by— with a Good Samaritan behind the wheel. If luck was on your side, you'd be able to tow the car to the nearest village and hunt down a mechanic who could work their magic and make the vehicle roadworthy again.

Life in the desert was simple for the locals, sustained mainly by the occasional farming of corn and *bajra*, crops that relied heavily on the unpredictable weather, or by selling the sheared wool from their sheep. Many seemed accustomed to a slow, almost lethargic pace of life, perhaps a reflection of the stillness around them.

Sandstorms, locally known as *Aandhi*, were frequent visitors during the scorching summers. Those storms carried fine sand from the surrounding dunes, forming a dense, swirling curtain in the air. At the first sign of it approaching, everyone would lock the doors and windows tightly, bracing for the storm's arrival. Even then, the fine sand always found its way inside, squeezing through the tiniest gaps. Once the storm passed, it left behind a layer of sand everywhere—on the roads, courtyards, and even inside homes. The aftermath meant at least two days of sweeping and clearing for the residents.

The larger sandstorms were particularly awe-inspiring, capable of moving entire dunes and dramatically altering the desert's landscape in the blink of an eye.

Someone once joked, '*There's no place on Earth where a Malayali hasn't set foot.*' True to the saying, even in the heart of the desert, there was one— *Rajan Chettan* from *Pathanamthitta*. He made the desert his permanent home, after his wife had secured a government job there.

He ran a small Kerala store, a treasure trove for the handful of *Keralites* in the area—mostly military personnel. His shop stocked the essentials that every Keralite craved: boiled rice, coconuts, raw bananas, banana chips, coconut oil, and even the iconic *Chandrika soap*. For those longing for a taste of home, he also brought in delicacies like *achappam* and *kuzhalappam*.

The quarter I was allotted came with a modest patch of empty space at the front and rear—both blank canvases covered in sand. Determined to bring some greenery to that arid landscape, I poured in my best efforts.

After much care and persistence, I managed to nurture a few Tecoma Stans (*Piliya plants*), their vibrant yellow blooms adding a splash of colour to the barren surroundings, along with a handful of hardy neem trees. Encouraged, I even attempted to grow a coconut tree. Sadly, the relentless, scorching desert summer proved too much for it, and it withered away under the unforgiving sun.

Weekends in the desert offered limited options for outings. Our usual destinations were a small rainwater pond and the endless sand dunes, which became favourite spots for our little ones. The kids loved tumbling and playing in the sand, their joy bringing life to the barren surroundings. However, their fun left its mark—puffs of sand would linger in the car and cling to our clothes, subtle reminders of our sandy escapades that seemed to follow us for days.

The small market in town was just enough to cater to basic needs. For anything beyond the essentials, we had to rely on Jodhpur. Thankfully, trips to Jodhpur were frequent, as people often travelled there for official purposes. All it took was keeping track of those journeys and requesting a favour to bring whatever we needed from the bustling markets there. One such item we frequently sourced was cakes—especially those meant for special occasions like birthdays.

Quarterly welfare meetings were a regular feature in every unit, providing a platform for personnel to voice concerns and seek solutions. Chaired by the Commander, those sessions were marked by active participation from all.

While not a formal rule, it was customary for senior officers to occupy the front row, with their deputies seated in the row behind them. The seating arrangement was typically hierarchical, with seniors, often needing to address queries, stuck in the front rows, while juniors, preferring to avoid the spotlight, opted for quiet spots in the last row.

During one such gathering, someone proposed the genuine need for a bakery at the station, and the suggestion was met with enthusiastic support from everyone in attendance.

The Commander, quick to act, decided to make it happen as a welfare measure. He asked his deputy in the front row, "Mugs, when can we have the bakery up and running?"

The deputy, knowing there was no option to decline, adopted a thoughtful expression for a moment before responding, "Sir, we can plan to have it functional in three weeks."

"Excellent. Gentlemen, the bakery will be inaugurated on the 25th of this month," the Commander declared decisively. The adjutant, ever meticulous, promptly noted the date in his diary.

The deputy then tilted his head toward the row behind him, locking eyes with his immediate junior officer, who instantly understood the unspoken directive and acknowledged with a nod. Those silent delegations continued down the chain of command, with each officer passing the responsibility backward with a subtle nod. Finally, it reached the last row, where the junior-most in the chain, Corporal Samy too gave a nod of acknowledgment. Realizing there were no more rows to pass it on, he understood that the responsibility for setting up the bakery now rested squarely on his shoulders.

Days seemed to fly by, and while Corporal Samy had made some initial efforts to set up the bakery, he faced roadblocks at various levels of the hierarchy. Soon, overwhelmed by other pressing tasks, the project was relegated to the bottom of his priority list.

Two days before the scheduled inauguration, the adjutant, ever punctual, referred to his diary and called the deputy commander to confirm the time for the ceremony. Only then did the deputy commander recall the bakery project, which had slipped his mind since the meeting. Alarmed, he contacted the officer to whom he had delegated the task. That sparked a chain reaction, as the task was passed down through the hierarchy until it reached Corporal Samy, who stood bewildered, unaware of the brewing storm.

The deputy commander, furious, reprimanded everyone involved and barked, "I don't care how you do it. The bakery must be functional on the 25th!"

Based on the confirmation from deputy, the adjutant issued a formal announcement: 'The bakery inauguration is scheduled for the 25th at 1700 hrs. All personnel, along with their spouses, are requested to attend.'

What followed was a flurry of activity on a war footing. Within an hour, a storage room in the shopping complex was cleared out, cleaned, and prepped for renovation. By evening, the room gleamed with a fresh coat of Sky Blue paint.

Tables and chairs were swiftly arranged, and glass enclosures essential for the bakery were sourced from the local market the following day. Meanwhile, a team was dispatched to Jodhpur at first light to procure bakery items—Fresh Bread, cakes, pastries, jaleby, laddoo, and a long list of other treats. The list seemed endless, but the mission was clear: the bakery would be ready, come what may.

On the morning of the 25th, the team began decorating the bakery with colourful paper streamers and glowing lights. A freshly made name board reading *Blue Sky Bakery* was installed at the entrance, adorned with flower garlands that added a festive charm. An inauguration plaque, engraved on a marble stone, was affixed to the wall and covered with a cloth curtain, ready to be unveiled during the ceremony.

By three in the afternoon, the team returned from Jodhpur with an assortment of baked goods. They carefully arranged *cakes, jalebis, laddoos*, and more in the sparkling glass enclosures, creating a delightful display. As the clock inched closer to five, the entire station gathered there eagerly.

The Commander arrived at five. After delivering a brief and gracious address, he officially declared the bakery open. His wife ceremonially cut the ribbon, while he unveiled the inauguration plaque, revealing the details inscribed proudly for all to see.

The Commander, visibly pleased with the efforts that brought the bakery to life, commended the team for their dedication and hard work. In his closing remarks, he extended heartfelt appreciation to all involved. To cap off the event, he presented Corporal Samy with a formal letter of appreciation, acknowledging his unwavering commitment and dedication in fulfilling the station's long-cherished dream.

TRANSFER CHRONICLES

A posting was always a challenge—a whirlwind of packing, relocating to an unfamiliar place, starting from scratch, and gradually finding your footing at the new place. For a soldier, the change was often straightforward; the work and routine remained similar, with only the faces changing. Thanks to the shared camaraderie of the uniform, those gaps were easily bridged. But for families, it was an entirely different story.

For school going children, the transition brought additional challenges—securing admission in a new school, often amidst stiff struggles. While the *Kendriya Vidyalayas* (KVs) were established to cater to the needs of personnel with transferable jobs, most of them were bursting at the seams, leaving many families to seek alternatives. As a result, often they had to settle for other schools in the vicinity. For the children it was a world of new teachers, classmates, and friendships. It naturally took time for kids to adapt to their new environment.

A typical posting lasted around three years, but the duration could vary widely, from a year and half to as long as four years, depending on the location and position. Prime postings in metros with good schools and robust connectivity were highly sought after, while remote or less desirable locations were avoided at all costs. At a godforsaken place, if luck isn't on your side, even those dealing with the postings might conveniently forget you and leave you stranded there until you remind them.

Once the posting order was issued, the new unit would send a joining instruction. Those invariably included the familiar disclaimer: *'There is an acute shortage of family accommodation at the moment. It is advisable to leave your family at your present station and move them over after finding alternate arrangements. Presently, a single accommodation has been arranged for you in the mess.'*

In over ten postings after our marriage, I never came across a joining instruction that declared family quarters were readily available!

It was just an advisory in most cases. Unless it was a non-family station—such as a remote or hostile area without basic amenities like quarters or schools—they couldn't have refused it. Despite all those cautions, I always chose to move with family. My philosophy was simple: *'Either they adjust and provide us some shelter, or we adjust and manage.'*

Of course, that wasn't without its share of difficulties. More often than not, we ended up living in a single room for months before moving into a temporary accommodation. For most wives, that arrangement wasn't too bothersome—they were secretly relieved to escape the daily grind of cooking, with mess dining taking that load off their shoulders. However, for husbands, the convenience came at a cost. Feeding a family of four at the mess often meant an eye-watering bill at the end of the month, sometimes swallowing up the entire salary!

Essential items like uniforms, a few essential clothes, and school books were carried along, while the bulk of the household belongings were packed into boxes and sent ahead in a hired truck. It would typically arrive within a few days and find shelter in an empty parking space or a vacant shed.

Packing household items was an art, carefully categorizing them based on their anticipated use at the new posting: 'immediate,' 'required,' and 'non essential.' Until a family quarter was allotted at the new unit, only the boxes labelled 'immediate' were opened—naturally, the one containing children's toys always makes it into the top priority category.

One might wonder why the 'non essential' items were even carried if they won't be used. For every fauji, certain belongings hold an emotional attachment—perhaps a showpiece purchased during a memorable posting, a gifted dinner set, or an outfit worn for a special occasion like a

'Husbands' Night' party. They were destined to remain part of his journey until retirement or even beyond that.

After a few weeks, if luck favoured you, a temporary home—a modest single-bedroom unit where the kitchen could be made functional—might be allotted to you. Everyone knew that arrangement was temporary, though in many cases, *'temporary'* ended up lasting for the better part of the posting. To avoid the hassle of another round of packing when shifting to an entitled quarter in due course, only the bare essentials were unpacked at the temporary home.

For the ladies, temporary quarters were hardly a joy. The brief reprieve of mess dining comes to an abrupt halt, replaced by the task of setting up a bare-bones kitchen with the few unpacked items.

It could take months before a proper quarter was finally allotted. The longer the wait, the more the packed items gradually found their way into the temporary home, turning it into a cluttered, cramped space that resembled a chaotic jumble. Moving boxes around during packing and unpacking could often lead to big surprises!

One morning, as I was getting ready for work, a frantic cry from the kitchen sent me rushing there. "Snake... SNAKE!" my wife screamed, pointing toward a corner of the room.

I spotted the intruder, but as I took a closer look, my heart skipped a beat—it was a baby cobra!

Both our kids also arrived at the scene, their eyes wide with curiosity. They all looked to me—the courageous soldier—to take charge of the situation. I didn't disappoint them. After a few tense moments, I managed to trap the cobra in a bag.

Then, a nagging thought crossed my mind— how on earth had a baby cobra made it to the fourth floor?

We were in for an even bigger shock when we looked around. A few packing boxes and wooden crates lay in the corridor, belonging to an officer who had recently moved into the quarter right across from mine. Upon inspecting them, we discovered two more baby cobras along with a few broken eggshells in one of the boxes!

A cobra had likely laid eggs inside the box while it was stored in the garage for nearly six months, awaiting quarter allotment. Later, when the boxes were brought indoors for unpacking, the eggs must have hatched.

Once the realization set in, panic rippled through everyone. Were there more lurking around? And worse—was the mother still nearby? To our relief, we found no more!

With officers arriving and departing continuously, the occupants of the quarters often changed, sometimes resulting in two or three officers moving in and out of the same quarter during one's stay at a station. Years later, when they met somewhere, it was common for them to reminisce about the good old days at their previous station. The conversation often turned to the whereabouts of others as well.

Two decades ago, while serving at a unit in the South, I had two colleagues whose wives, whom we respectfully addressed as *Bindu Madam* and *Raji Madam*, became close friends. Eventually, both of them were posted to different units, but their wives kept in touch over the phone. Years later, the ladies had a chance meeting during a vacation in Kochi. They talked for hours, fondly remembering the wonderful time they had together in their old unit.

An officer who had served with them at that unit, had sadly passed away sometime back. Raji had heard about it from her husband and thought of sharing it with Bindu during their conversation. Though she couldn't recall the officer's name, she mentioned that he used to live in the quarters adjacent to where Bindu lived. Bindu knew him vaguely, but she also couldn't recollect the name. After catching up for about an hour, they exchanged goodbyes and parted ways.

Soon after reaching home, Bindu called her husband in Kolkata and shared the news using the same reference that

Raji had mentioned. Her husband immediately identified the officer in question—an Army Signal Officer who had served in their unit. Wasting no time, he passed on the news to another officer who also had been with them in Trivandrum. He took it a step further, spreading the news to everyone he could think of. Soon, the news reached their old unit too.

Since the officer in question was from the Army having absolutely no contact with the Air Force guys ever since he left, none had any update on him as well. Everyone who heard the tragic news, was deeply saddened.

A little while later, they managed to track down his spouse's contact number, and a senior officer from the old unit called her to express his condolences. To his astonishment, she immediately handed the phone to her husband. Realizing something was terribly amiss, the senior officer found himself fumbling for words. After a brief apology and an awkward chat, he hung up, thoroughly embarrassed.

Before the senior officer could act, many others had already called to convey their condolences as well. Thankfully, the officer in question, assuming it was just a prank, played along with good humour.

In reality, the unfortunate death had occurred—but it wasn't the Army officer. It was an officer who had lived in the same quarters before the Army family moved in. Raji's information to Bindu was accurate, but Bindu's husband mistakenly presumed it to be the next occupant, that triggered the entire drama. Entire confusion arose from the frequent rotation of occupants in the quarters, where one often sees a succession of neighbours over time.

A little later, I too called the Army colleague, and he answered with a chuckle, "Hello, Mats. I assume you're calling to offer condolences, right? Thank you very much!" By then, I knew the real story and explained the mix-up. We shared a hearty laugh, and before hanging up, I added with a grin, "Wishing you a long, healthy second life, Sir!"

HOLLOW LEADERS

Leadership in the military is a profound responsibility, demanding unwavering integrity and commitment. A true leader must serve as an inspiring role model for their subordinates, leading by example through words and actions.

The cherished mantra carried in every soldier's heart—'Service before Self'—should resonate in every decision a leader makes, motivating others to follow in their footsteps. During my military career, I had the privilege of working with many such exceptional leaders who inspired everyone to strive for excellence and emulate their example.

Remarkable leaders exist across all walks of life—whether in politics, the military, government, private institutions, or sports. However, exceptions do exist. Some individuals preach ideals but fail to reflect them in their actions, eroding the trust and principles they were meant to uphold.

The military, as a reflection of society, is not immune to such shortcomings. On very rare occasions, I have encountered a few leaders who abandoned their principles and displayed opportunistic behaviour.

While posted in Srinagar, a few of us were to accompany our Commander on a visit to an Army unit in a remote, militancy-affected village. A Tata Sumo was arranged for our journey, while the Commander was expected to lead us in his staff car. Both vehicles had the armed escorts, as mandated.

Our Commander was known for following protocol even while travelling. He always preferred to travel comfortably seated alone at the rear seat of his staff car, while inside the station.

That day, however, he surprised us all. Instead of his usual routine, he walked straight to the Sumo and took the centre seat in the middle row. He had two officers seated on either side of him, while another two and an armed escort squeezed into the rear cabin. I was asked to share the front passenger seat with another armed escort. Despite his obvious discomfort in the cramped middle seat, he assured us that he was perfectly fine. We were genuinely touched by our commanders that humble gesture.

Cautiously, we set out for the Army unit, and by the grace of God, nothing untoward happened on the way. The seating arrangement remained unchanged on the return trip as well.

However, the moment we reached the safe confines of the camp, the Commander quickly reverted to his usual self—the one who meticulously followed every protocol. His unusual behaviour left us all puzzled. That's when a witty colleague offered a possible explanation: "Maybe he was worried about militants targeting the vehicle. Sitting in the middle seat, he had human shields protecting him from the front, back, and both sides!"

There were leaders who captivate their audience with powerful, inspiring speeches, yet rarely practice what they preach. The military, too, has its share of such individuals.

In the desert, water was always scarce, but one particularly harsh summer brought an even more severe shortage. Despite the administration's best efforts, the water transported in bowsers from distant locations was barely sufficient.

One morning, during the daily unit parade, the Commander delivered an emotional speech about the importance of conserving precious water. He enthusiastically urged everyone to adopt measures like 'bathing with just a single mug of water' and other frugal practices. His words struck a chord, and the troops committed to following his advice diligently.

That evening, however, I happened to see a water bowser drive into the Commander's courtyard. As soon as it stopped, a helper rushed forward, opened the outlet valve, and began lavishly watering the lawn and plants. Within moments, the tanker was empty, and the driver hurried off to fetch another load to finish the job.

As I stood watching that scene unfold, I couldn't help but recall the Commander's rousing speech from the morning and reflect on the stark contradiction between his words and actions.

Most soldiers carry a serious demeanor, especially in front of their subordinates. Like a rare rainbow on the horizon, seeing a smile on their face is an uncommon sight.

In Trivandrum, there was a senior officer who epitomized this stern persona. He had twenty subordinates, myself included, and none of us had ever witnessed even a hint of a smile. His face was always a reflection of seriousness and often anger.

Once he attended a workshop on *'Happiness in Life'*, conducted by a renowned spiritual Guru. Perhaps inspired by the session, the following day we saw something extraordinary—a rare smile on his face. As he concluded the briefing, he encouraged everyone to start each day with a smile, a suggestion that brought a rare sense of cheer to us.

The next morning, as we entered his office for the briefing, we all saluted and greeted him with smiles, remembering his words from the day before. We hoped for a return of our smiles.

But instead, he snapped, "Why the f*** are you all smiling? Do I look like a joker here?" His voice roared, as his anger flared up once again.

Whatever magic the spiritual Guru had worked on him had clearly evaporated in just one day.

An old saying came to my mind at that moment: *'You can never straighten a dog's tail, no matter how hard you try.'*

MILITARY PARTIES

No military tale is ever complete without a hearty mention of the spirited social gatherings that breathe life into the forces. Amidst the laughter and camaraderie, the invisible leash of rank, protocol, and tradition ensures that even the most laid-back parties have an air of polished formality.

Every unit has its unique ways of celebrating, and in the armed forces, few gatherings are as iconic as the '*Rum Punch*' and the '*Badakhana.*' Whether it's the unit anniversary, Air Force Day, or the culmination of a major milestone, these events seamlessly blend tradition with festivity, keeping the spirit of togetherness alive.

'Rum Punch' is a classic evening bash, where the clinking of glasses, hearty laughter, and an array of snacks create the perfect recipe for camaraderie. Meanwhile, the 'Badakhana' is a grand lunch, often attended by spouses and kids.

The Officers' Mess is a lively hub of activity, hosting everything from casual Tambola nights to formal gatherings held on occasions like Air Force Day or during the Dining-In and Dining-Out of officers. The formal events were steeped in ceremonial elegance, with officers adorned in the mess uniforms of the season.

Those gatherings were more than just parties; they were cherished traditions, seamlessly blending celebration with the core values of respect, order, and unity that define the armed forces. Though the format was inherently formal, those events often provided moments of entertainment.

During my posting in Trivandrum, an Air Force Day dinner was hosted at the Officers' Mess—a grand occasion exuding formal elegance and camaraderie. The evening's chief guest was the Governor of Kerala, accompanied by an array of dignitaries from the state government and other branches of the armed forces.

To add a cultural flourish to the evening, someone suggested showcasing Kerala's renowned traditional art forms, *Kathakali* and *Kalaripayattu*. The Commander, a North Indian with little familiarity with those artistic treasures, was instantly intrigued and gave his enthusiastic approval. A troupe from a local art school was promptly hired to bring those iconic performances to life on stage.

The Commander knew that the Governor would leave early after spending about thirty minutes in the party. As he was required to deliver a formal address to thank the guests, he directed that the entertainment segment be limited to fifteen minutes, ensuring he could complete his address before the Chief Guest's departure.

The event unfolded on schedule, with the Governor arriving dot on time. After the customary Air Force Song, the entertainment began with *Kathakali*. The performance started with *Purapadu*, a ritual where a curtain is held at the front to conceal the artist.

Unfortunately, the curtain used that evening was a sorry sight—faded, tattered, and no match to the military standards of perfection. The Commander's displeasure was very evident.

The *Kathakali* performance stretched well beyond the total allocated time, fraying the Commander's patience. It was soon conveyed to the artist, who reluctantly wound up the show and exited the stage.

Before the Commander could take the stage for his address, the *Kalaripayattu* team seized the spotlight. With swords and other weapons in hand, they launched into a spirited demonstration of their art. Probably, realizing the risks of interrupting performers wielding sharp weapons, the Commander decided to move away—though his growing impatience was obvious.

As the Governor's departure approached, the Commander issued firm orders to wrap up the performance. The coordinators sprang into action, attempting to halt the show. However, the performers, fully immersed in their routine, ignored the signals. The coordinators resorted to physically pulling away the artists who ventured near the stage's edge during their mock combat.

Gradually, all but the lead performer were removed. Realizing he was the last man standing with no 'opponent' left to fight, the lead artist too reluctantly bowed out. Seizing the moment, the Commander delivered a concise two-line thank-you note and ensured the Governor's departure went smoothly.

The following day, however, was far from smooth for the coordinators. The Commander vented his frustration over the '*dirty bedsheet masquerading as a curtain*' and the inability to control the performers.

The evening remained a fondly remembered tale of how cultural fervour and military discipline can sometimes collide in the most amusing ways.

While the dress code in the messes was usually formal, there were occasions when the atmosphere turned refreshingly relaxed, with everyone embracing casual or even whimsical costumes. One such event was Husband's Night, where the ladies took on the role of hosts for the fauji husbands.

The party will have a theme. A '*Chambal Night*' might see the venue transformed into a forest hideout, complete with decor evoking a dacoit's den. Guests arrive dressed as bandits or outlaws, brandishing toy weapons or replicas, making for an evening of laughter, camaraderie, and creative flair!

Since those themed parties happened every year, everyone would have been part of many such events during their service life with creative themes like '*Bhojpuri*', '*Bollywood*', '*Arabian Nights*', and more.

To match the themes of those numerous parties, many even went as far as purchasing outfits specifically for the occasion.

Once the event was over, those costumes would find a quiet corner in their wardrobes, eventually ending up in a trunk dedicated to such fancy dress items.

The fun didn't stop at the costumes and makeup. The so-called guests at those parties were required to make a grand entrance, often re-enacting a famous scene from an old blockbuster movie besides performing a brief skit to entertain the hosts – the ladies!

I usually steered clear of stage performances—be it acting or dancing—by cleverly taking on responsibilities like managing the audio-visual setup or attending to guests, always making sure to appear busy. It was my tried-and-tested escape plan. Yet, despite my best efforts, I found myself roped into the action on two occasions.

The first was in Mumbai during an Air Force anniversary celebration, where someone had the bright idea to organize a fashion show featuring various Air Force uniforms. With no way to escape, I reluctantly donned one of the mess uniforms and performed a catwalk on stage—a fashion debut I'd rather not repeat!

The second occasion was in Trivandrum during a Husband's Night, where our team decided to perform a skit spoofing the iconic Titanic movie. Our entry to the beachside party venue was nothing short of unforgettable.

I played Jack, while a colleague portrayed Rose wearing a long gown and other costumes. Standing at the tip of a boat in the famous Titanic pose, we recreated the scene as our commander sat behind us, holding a fake helm, with Celine Dion's *'My Heart Will Go On..'* playing in the background.

Fortunately, the boat didn't capsize; otherwise, the climax we had planned with a twist for the stage might have unfolded right there in the water!

SUBTLE GOODBYES

Wearing the uniform is a privilege earned through immense effort, and relinquishing it prematurely can be just as daunting. While officers commissioned under short service are permitted to step away after completing their stipulated tenure, those with a permanent commission are traditionally expected to serve until retirement.

Premature exits are allowed but only under exceptional circumstances, requiring approval from Service Headquarters—a process that is both rigorous and demanding.

Many young individuals join the military without much deliberation. However, during the intense training, it's not uncommon for some to question their decision and start contemplating an early exit.

A few others may arrive at a similar decision later, once they are posted to units in remote corners of the vast country. Once such thoughts take root, they would start exploring ways to leave.

Applications for release often cite reasons that range from straightforward concerns, such as the need to support aging parents, to more complex challenges, like a spouse's demand for divorce due to difficulties adjusting to military life. If the case was genuine, Headquarters would generally review it with compassion.

Yet, not all cases were straightforward. Some individuals, tempted by better career opportunities elsewhere, would concoct questionable reasons to secure their release.

A few on the other hand, unwilling to endure the lengthy formalities, take a shortcut and vanish without even a trace. They disappear on an ordinary morning, leaving no clue about their whereabouts. Often, even their closest allies remain unaware until they fail to return after a long vacation.

In such cases, a police inquiry is initiated, but they were clever enough to relocate to distant places, sometimes even other countries. Branded as 'Deserters,' efforts to track them continue for ever. Notifications would go to various government agencies, including the passport office, making the risk of being apprehended significantly high.

Fearing such consequences, not many would dare to attempt such a drastic step. For most, following the official process to secure approval remains the only viable path. Yet, there were those who realized that conventional grounds wouldn't work in their favour and instead resorted to creative, sometimes cunning, ways to achieve their goal.

During his engineering studies, young Thomas—Tomy, as his friends called him—a native of Kerala, dreamed of securing a lucrative job in the Middle East. Fate, however, had other plans for him. He was selected for the engineering stream in Indian Air Force, where he joined soon after his graduation.

While training in Bangalore, he gradually adapted to the military routine. Weekends were spent exploring the city with college friends who had moved there in search of stable jobs. Watching their struggles, Thomas began to feel that his decision to join the Air Force had been the right one.

However, the rosy phase ended when his first posting took him to an IAF unit situated in a remote corner of West Bengal. Having grown accustomed to the comforts and liveliness of Bangalore, the desolate location left him deeply disheartened.

As time passed, many of his friends found success, settling in the Middle East and US with glamorous jobs. Thomas, meanwhile, felt trapped in an isolated corner of the country.

His only solace was his weekend trips to Kolkata, where he indulged in movies, pubs, and good food. Despite those escapes, the dream of Dubai often haunted him. He applied for release from service, but his request was promptly rejected.

During one of his visits to Calcutta, he heard about a charity organization run by missionaries. Intrigued, he visited the organization and was deeply moved by what he saw there.

He began volunteering there every weekend, finding solace in serving the poor and underprivileged. For nearly a year, he dedicated his weekends to charity work, except when service commitments required his presence elsewhere. In time, he even had the opportunity to interact with the head of the missionaries. Noticing his dedication, she once asked why he hadn't considered joining the organization full-time.

Thomas explained his military obligations, but when she asked if he was truly interested in dedicating himself to charity, his answer was a heartfelt '*Yes.*'

A week later, Thomas was summoned by his commanding officer and asked to submit an application for release. Surprised, he guessed it might have been the result of his conversation with the head of the missionaries. He complied, and soon his request was approved without a hitch.

Unbeknownst to him, the head of the missionaries had reached out to higher-ups in the government, requesting to consider his release to serve her organization. Moved by the sincerity of her appeal, the authorities granted the unusual request.

Soon, Thomas left the service and joined the charity organization. For almost a year, he worked tirelessly as a full-time volunteer, finding fulfilment in his work. But as time passed, his long-cherished dream of Dubai resurfaced, stronger than ever.

With a heavy heart, he informed the organization of his decision to leave, as he no longer felt the same enthusiasm he once had.

Soon, Thomas made his way to Dubai, achieving the dream he had carried for so long—albeit through a detour that had profoundly shaped his journey.

ADIEU TO SALUTES

Bidding farewell is never easy. For a soldier, though, it's a ritual woven into the fabric of service life—a rhythm of departures and arrivals that becomes second nature over time. Each posting ends with goodbyes, handshakes, and promises to stay in touch. At first, my final send-off felt no different, just another chapter closing. But deep down, I knew that was unlike any farewell before. The weight of it didn't hit me immediately; it crept in slowly over the following few days.

That night, as I donned my uniform for the last time, a tidal wave of emotions washed over me—pride, gratitude, and an undeniable pang of loss. The uniform, my second skin for twenty-five years, had shielded me, shaped me, and been a symbol of all I stood for. Its stripes, medals, and badges told a story of dedication, sacrifice, and countless memories. That night marked the end of an extraordinary journey, and with it came the daunting uncertainty of what lay ahead.

At the farewell party, someone asked, "Why did you decide to leave?" The question lingered, giving me pause for reflection. Was it the relentless cycle of relocations every few years that had finally taken its toll? As the years passed and age steadily climbed, the once-thrilling adventure of packing up and starting anew had become more draining, with both mind and body struggling to keep pace.

Or perhaps it was the growing realization that my children's youth years were slipping through my fingers. I probably feared becoming a mere visitor in their lives, a distant figure with fond but fleeting memories.

May be it was the freedom that I enjoyed during my younger days, the laughter and energy that once lit up every duty, now dulled by the mere repetition of days fuelled by the weight of not so thrilling and adventurous senior responsibilities that lacked avenues for creativity.

Or was it the creeping monotony of routine, the sense of treading familiar paths with little left to conquer? I didn't have a straight answer, just fragments of reasons that together formed the picture of my decision.

Then came the inevitable follow-up: "What's next?" I smiled, masking the unease that flickered within. The love for the uniform had consumed me so completely that I'd rarely allowed myself to imagine life beyond it. A few opportunities awaited, but I hadn't embraced them yet. First, I needed to come to terms with the reality of stepping out of the life that had defined me for so long.

Retiring at an age when others were still climbing career ladders felt strange. Was I truly ready, or was I allowing this transition to age me before my time? Those questions lingered as the night unfolded.

I knew I would soon be embracing my real name, Sunil, once again after so many years. In the forces, everyone knew me by my second name, Mathews, naturally assuming it was my surname. Over time, it morphed into the shorter and more convenient 'Mats,' a name I grew to love. As a nod to my younger, more energetic self, I decided to keep it as my pen name—if I ever venture into serious writing!

As I looked back on my years in the Air Force, a wave of gratitude swept over me. It wasn't just a career; it was an odyssey—one filled with thrilling adventures, unshakable friendships, daunting challenges, and countless little triumphs that felt monumental in the moment. The Air Force didn't merely give me a job; it gave me a purpose, a home where camaraderie thrived, and a treasure trove of memories that will forever be etched in my heart. Truly, it has been a life like no other—a journey that shaped me, tested me, and gave me stories worth telling for a lifetime.

It was an incredible experience, walking shoulder to shoulder with people from different faiths and regions, bound by a common purpose. We weren't just a mix of people from across the country—we were a team. We respected each other for who we were, remained focused on our shared mission, and stood by one another through every challenge. It reinforced what we already knew—the true essence of our nation's spirit: Unity in Diversity.

Thankfully, my final farewell that night lacked formal speeches —a tradition abandoned long ago. No obligatory flattery from a commander offering praise laced with formality, no drawn-out lists of thanks and apologies. I welcomed the simplicity.

Yet, some customs endure—like the presentation of a memento. A small but meaningful token of one's bond with the unit, it symbolizes the journey shared. That night, I received not just the unit memento but also the Indian Air Force memento—the final parting gift. Soon, they would find their place on my living room wall, silently telling tales of duty, honour, and service.

As I hung my uniform in the wardrobe that night, I felt a mix of excitement and trepidation about what's next. The road ahead felt uncharted, but one thing was certain: the lessons and values forged over the last twenty-five years would light my way forward. I knew with every step forward, I would carry the spirit of the uniform within me, ready to face whatever comes on the way.

If time could turn back and I were once again a young man standing at the crossroads of choice, I wouldn't hesitate for a moment to proudly don the beautiful blue uniform once more—ready to serve with the same passion and enthusiasm, savouring every moment of the wonderful journey all over again!

नभः स्पृशं दीप्तम्
Touch the Sky with Glory

ACKNOWLEDGEMENT

A journey spanning 25 years in the military is not just about duty and discipline—it's about the people who make it unforgettable. Every interaction, regardless of rank or position, has shaped my experiences, and each of you has been a part of this story in one way or another. While it's impossible to name everyone who has left an impact, I wouldn't be at peace without mentioning a few who come to mind.

To *Rajesh, Ajay, Prashanth, Venky, Santhosh, Rajiv, KVS, Atul, Arun, Javed, Raju,* and *Sasi*—my partners in crime during those unforgettable training days.

To *Samir, Lakhpat,* and *Biju,* three wonderful souls who left us too soon—you are remembered with fondness and gratitude.

To *Goparaju, Abdesh Jha, Sriharsha, Sood, Wadhwa,* and *Mishy,* who made our Delhi days full of laughter and camaraderie.

To *Kalia, Hari Sir, Prateek, Shibu, Ashok Sir,* and *Khurmi Sir,* who brought light and laughter into our bachelor days.

To *Mahi, Manesh, Sajeev, Manoj, Rajesh, Soumitro, Syam, RSM,* and *Vishy Sir,* who ensured my wife mastered her culinary skills during our days in the valley!

To *Mohan Sir & Mala Ma'am, Subash Sir, Pradeep Sir & Sujatha Ma'am, Menon Sir & Bindu Ma'am, Hari Sir & Rashmi Ma'am,* who turned confinement into a time of warmth and friendship.

To *Dinesh, Shibu, Sharath, Kajuria, Bhuyi, Sumal,* and *Mohit Sir,* who added spirit and energy to our days in Mumbai.

To *Kapil, Gaurav, Rohit, Dubey Sir, Sarkar Sir, Dave, Dasgupta, Paldikar, Jinendar, Kashyaps,* and *Gudads,* who braved the sandstorms together.

To *Sony Sir, Jayachandran, Pramod, Punnose Sir, Tomy Sir, Rajendran Sir, George Sir, Joe,* and *Amal*, for standing together through the storms in Trivandrum.

To my mentors and bosses—Rajinder Sir, Amit Sir, Alok Sir, Gupta Sir, Brar Sir, Hari Sir and many others—for imparting wisdom and guidance at various levels of my career, shaping me into the person I am today.

To *Indrajith, Sreekumar, Shiva, Joby, Minhas, Ranaji, Sundar,* and *Ratish*—just a few from my endless list of colleagues—thank you for your unwavering support and encouragement, which boosted my confidence in writing.

To my brother-in-law, *Teny*, a brilliant writer himself, and my dear friends *Manoj* and *Sujatha Ma'am*, for proofreading this book and offering invaluable insights.

To *Sreekumar*, whose vast experience in print and media provided crucial guidance in shaping the reach of this book.

To my nephew, *Arun Joji*, for lending his creative touch to the beautiful cover design.

And finally, to my wife, *Gino*, and our sons, *Rohan* and *Rohit*, whose unwavering support and belief in me gave me the strength to complete this book.

Each of you, through your presence, support, and memories, has left an imprint on every page of this book. Thank you!